I0439475

GREED IS GOOD
BIG IS BAD

How to Fix America's Problems

MICHAEL ENGMANN

First Published 2014
Copyright © 2014 Michael W. Engmann. All Rights Reserved.

ACKNOWLEDGMENTS

I am extremely thankful for the blessings bestowed upon me. The love and affection of my parents, my wife and two sons, and my other family members have been my treasure. They have fueled the belief in myself that drives my ambition to be a better person. One of the greatest gifts of life is the fulfillment of one's self-esteem. And, this must be nurtured with a loving family. I have been lucky to have such a wonderful family.

I am also extremely fortunate to be living in America where the opportunity to succeed wasn't limited as I pursued my dreams. Many wars were fought by the citizens of this country to preserve the gift of freedom and the political and economic setting to allow dreams to come true. Americans owe everything to those brave soldiers who sacrificed for the future of this country. I am immensely grateful. I thank all this country's veterans and their families for all their blood, sweat, and tears.

—*Michael Engmann*

CONTENTS

CONTENTS

INTRODUCTION

America is going down a long dark path. We've managed to climb out of seemingly desperate economic situations before. But unless we act and change, America may no longer be the best-loved, freedom-based country on earth – a country where most people in the world would love to live. This book will shed some light on America's current struggles and why 'power' has become dangerously consolidated in 'big government', 'big business', and 'big labor'. Also, our politicians have created an 'encyclopedia' of laws specifically designed to control most aspects of our lives. This is the antithesis of what our Founding Fathers designed and dreamed about for our nation.

One thing that American ancestry was most proud of was the ability and the responsibility to provide for themselves and their children. Government was only expected to keep the American 'Dream' (the path of freedom and the pursuit of happiness) alive. Times have changed. Today, at least 50% of Americans are dependent on some kind of government subsidy (food stamps, sec. 8 housing, school lunches, Obama cell phones, etc.). Today, Americas are taught that the government should do everything from health care to resolving wealth discrepancies to governing its citizens' sugar intake!

INTRODUCTION

This is not the America our forefathers or pre-baby boomers envisioned. Our Constitution has served us well for over 200 years. We must return to its original intent, protect it and honor those who gave their lives in its service. True Americans need to bring their fight to battle against false politician promises and the 'blob' the government has become!

The Original Purpose of America's Government – How Far Have We Strayed?

The original purpose of American government according to our founding fathers can be seen in their writing of the Preamble of the Constitution. The Preamble of the Constitution states -

"We the People of the United States, in Order to form a more perfect Union, establish Justice, insure domestic Tranquility, provide for the common defence, promote the general Welfare, and secure the Blessings of Liberty to ourselves and our Posterity, do ordain and establish this Constitution for the United States of America".

This Preamble states the main six goals our founding fathers wanted to achieve for the new nation of America. The first goal of forming a more "perfect Union" became important when our founding fathers recognized problems arising out of the Articles of Confederation and Perpetual State establishing the United States in 1776. The federal government had originally been given no ability to raise money. It also had been given very little power over the behavior of the States in the Confederation. This had led to each State creating policies and laws regarding domestic and foreign commerce and ignoring their obligations to the Union regardless of the impact on the other States and the Union in general. Our founding fathers recognized that the only way the new nation could survive and prosper was to have a unified nation. A new foundation had to be laid to create a more powerful central government. The benefits of this new central government would outweigh the loss of some power to the States.

The second goal of the Constitution to "establish Justice" was based on the understanding that fair and equal treatment of the people by a government's laws would create the strongest of nations with the greatest satisfaction of its citizens.

The third goal to "insure domestic Tranquility" concerned creating laws and policy that would insure differences of opinions and interests mostly between states could be resolved in a legal manner vs. a violent manner.

The fourth goal of the Constitution to "provide for the common defence" was based on the understanding that other nations of the world would be tempted to try to conquer the United States. In order to prevent this action, American government needed the authority to create a system to deter and respond to any such action.

The fifth goal to "promote the general Welfare" was directed at government's involvement in the coinage of money, taxation of commerce, handling issues between states, international dealings with foreign countries and with public policy concerning public lands. Our founders were most concerned with the infringement of citizens' rights but understood a strong country required that the central government created policy that would bind the citizens and states closer together.

The last goal "to secure the Blessings of Liberty to ourselves and our Posterity" was important to our founders as they were students of the history of government. The lesson they had learned was that all governments became usurpers of power. Regardless of citizens' initial rights in newly formed governments, government had always severely infringed on these rights with the passage of time. "Give me liberty or give me death" was a quotation which clearly reflected the thoughts of our founding fathers. It was their intention to create a foundation for government in which citizens' rights were unalterable.

To summarize the purpose of government, according to the ideas of our founding fathers, is to create an environment of liberty for its citizens. Our government was not expected to create new industries or new products. Production was left up to the private sector. And, the standard of living of citizens of the United States was not the purview of the government. Our forefathers understood that differences of opinions and interests would occur between individuals in a united society and would also occur between competing societies. The Constitution was a document that created a method for dealing with those different interests without giving additional powers to the government that would (immediately or eventually) compromise the freedom of individuals.

A brief review of the evolution of government and the history of government should provide an understanding of why our forefathers felt so strongly about freedom and minimizing the power of government.

At the most basic level, the purpose of government is to protect its citizens from foreign threats and provide its citizens with rules, regulation, and enforcement that restricts their behavior to that which is accepted by those who become its subjects.

From the beginning of time, people banded together for protection and because they needed the services of each other, whether emotional or economic. Hunting was more efficient in a group and the other tasks such as cooking, making tools and clothes and a living shelter became more productive in a tribe whose members had different skill sets. Rules concerning individual conduct (job tasks and individual social behavior) along with adjudication and enforcement were needed and implemented to create the conformity needed for tribe survival. Rules concerning the distribution of goods (food, shelter, trinkets) and mating were heavily weighted according to input by the strongest or most skilled hunters who provided food and protection for the tribe. They were the leaders and they determined the tribe's governance.

The tribe needed harmony to survive but even in the smallest of tribes, there was always some discontent. One or more of the tribe members always felt mistreated to some extent (Surprisingly in wealthy America today, virtually every family has issues of discontentment with members feeling mistreated even though current life would be considered heaven by the ancients. The driving force of human nature is unhappiness with the current condition. It is the cause of goods things such as advancements in science and technology and the cause of bad things such as persecution and wars). The degree of harmony in the tribe affected its success in survival, its power and the standard of living of its core members (Similar to team sports, harmony is more important than individual prowess in determining success). The interplay of the tribe's economic wellbeing (success in hunting, gathering, and security) and the feelings regarding fair treatment of tribe members determined the harmony of the tribe and also the anointment of the leader of the tribe.

In the tribe setting, governance was held in the tribal leaders' hands. The leadership position could be changed by general discontentment of the tribe. As tribes joined together to form communities, more disparate interests were produced and it became harder for community members to unite to replace leadership. And, when the community became large enough to support a standing army controlled by the leadership, the task of reshuffling, because of community discontentment, those in power became almost impossible. The link between harmony of the tribe (or people) and those who governed the tribe became much weaker. And, the abuse of power for the increased benefit of the leadership was vastly increased. In fact, the overwhelming majority of history concerns the oppression of the general populace in favor of the aristocratic ruling class.

In the tribal setting, governance was not complicated. Power was given to rulers (governors) to create rules that would achieve harmony in the tribe. Since these rulers could be removed, the system produced a positive feedback system that allowed progressive change to occur. With the formation of communities (hunting, farming, and commerce), and city states, the feedback system became much weaker and much less favorable to change. Early examples are civilizations founded in the Fertile Crescent, the Egyptian empires, and the Roman Empire. These civilizations were constantly at war for the benefit of the ruling class. And leadership of these civilizations was always controlled by the aristocratic class.

After the Roman Empire fell, in feudal times might was right as citizen protection was a critically needed commodity. Protection was afforded by the strong lord who became the head of the government of his protectorate. The amalgamation of protectorates lead to the aristocratic order with kings and queens at its helm. The power of the king's army and his political alliance with his associated aristocracy created a dictatorship which greatly benefited those in power at the expense of the general population. The aristocracy determined that the purpose of government was to benefit the aristocracy. And, laws, rules and regulations were instituted with that purpose in mind. Although the general population realized their plight (they were at the mercy of the aristocracy), they could do almost nothing to change it. And, the aristocratic governance lasted over 1000 years.

The question of what is the purpose of government cannot be answered without deciding what segment of the population seeks to control government. Kings thought the purpose of government was to fulfill their needs (the peasants didn't matter). Religious groups (fanatics) think the purpose of government is to make people conform to the rules of God. Political groups think the purpose of government is follow their ideology. History shows that powerful groups fight to mold the purpose of government to match their objectives. Historically, most governments have not been controlled by the general populace. Therefore, the rights of individuals had been of little concern to those in power. Our forefathers, as students of history, were well aware of this problem for the masses. As libertarians, they wrote the Constitution and the Bill of Rights to ensure the power of American government would not become authoritative.

In the two hundred plus years since the writing of the Constitution, the interpretation of its purpose has changed. In the last 50 years, the change has been dramatic. With this change, government has become very involved in the private lives of Americans and in how the economy is run. The new interpretation by the liberals governing America today can be seen in a recent Buzzle article.

In that article the basic purposes of government are laid out as follows.

"Government is the governing body of a nation. It is formed with an intent of establishing law and order in the society. What are the main purposes of a government?

Government is the governing authority of a political unit. The government of a nation is the ruling power as also the apparatus by the means of which the governing officials exercise authority. People need to lead a social life but a community cannot thrive without law and order. Society needs to be directed and should be based on a commonly accepted set of principles. This is briefly, what a governing authority does. A Government is also responsible for an overall welfare of the society and should ideally strive to bring about reforms in the society. The fundamental purpose of a government is to maintain basic security and public order.

The government plays a vital role in developing an economic security in the society. The country's economy has a direct effect on the lifestyle and quality of living of its inhabitants. Governments are created for increasing the people's potential for survival. Preventing the undermining of the nation's currency and regulating the economy of the country are thus the main responsibilities of a government. Government intends to stabilize the nation's economy for the benefit of its people.

The establishment of social security, which is closely related to economic security, is also an important purpose of the formation of a government. The government shares the responsibility of the senior citizens of society. The social security policies of the government result in the reduction in the poverty in society. Its provision of financial support to the elderly gives people a social security.

Guarding the country's border is the primary responsibility of a government. The purpose of the government is to create and maintain a vigilant force to safeguard the country. Governments create militaries with the purpose of defending the nation against its enemies. The government hosts the army, naval and air forces, which are responsible for protecting their motherland from any attack by the rival countries.

INTRODUCTION

The preservation of life and protection of property are also among the main purposes of a government. The maintenance of environmental goods and the preservation of a country's natural wealth is also an important purpose. It is the government's responsibility to resolve conflicts that arise on issues related to public goods and constituents of the environment.

One of the basic purposes of a government is to plan for the development of the nation. Providing the inhabitants of a country with the basic goods like public transport mechanisms, highways, health facilities as well as schools and educational institutions, is the responsibility of the government. It also aims at helping in the preservation of environment through the development of national parks and wildlife sanctuaries.

The other purpose of a government is, the establishment of equality and justice in society. The formation of certain rules that define the law and order of a nation are pillars of the social well-being of its people. Establishing rules and ensuring that they are followed is an important duty of a government. The government forms a governing authority that can be trusted by the masses. The purpose behind the establishment of a government is the formation of an authority that can guide the society.

It is the government that binds us together and helps us live in peace and harmony."

This article written by Manali Oak for Buzzle.com can be found at Buzzle:

http://www.buzzle.com/articles/basic-purposes-of-a-government.html.

INTRODUCTION

The difference reflected by the ideas of our founding fathers and modern interpretations of the role of government are substantial. In the case of our founding fathers, reliance on the government was abhorred. In the case of today's liberal interpretation, it is the government's role to be the guardian of the people. Since an essential element of freedom is self-reliance, the reliance on government must necessarily restrict freedom. And, the degree to which freedom is restricted is determined by the degree of reliance. In this liberal interpretation, government plays a very significant role in taking care of the individual. Liberty and freedom therefore lose significance in this viewpoint of the role of government.

The reduction in liberty and freedom seems to be justified by the liberal's assumption that government's role will produce a greater positive impact on society than the negative impact from the loss in the degree of freedom. This assumption is very questionable. Although new services are being introduced by the government, they have a cost. First, they require a redistribution of wealth. The negative impact from this action is not even considered. Since the government doesn't produce physical goods, it must buy them from the private sector to pay for the administration and other costs of the programs it implements. This causes resources to be diverted away from production and into administration. Production is therefore harmed. Also, a policy of taxing workers is needed to fund these programs. The policy of taxation creates a disincentive to produce and therefore is likely to cause overall production to decline. This jeopardizes government programs that rely on a certain societal level of production. The likely reduction in overall production, the overall loss of liberty and freedom, and the discrimination against the worker in favor of the non-worker make the liberal's assumptions that an increased governmental role in society is beneficial not credible.

So, what should be the role of American government? According to our founding fathers' interpretation, we are well outside of the Constitution's boundaries. Voters have moved us to the current state of government dependence as politicians have promised government 'freebies' and advocated for a bigger and bigger government every year since the Great Depression. As discussed, these 'freebies' have a significant cost.

Americans are giving up their freedom and locking themselves into a massive power structure. Belief that heavy government reliance is good and those in power will act in the best interests of the governed historically has been proven ill advised. America's current economic situation shows our current political system is no exception. Our government is currently 17 trillion dollars in debt and running a one trillion dollar a year deficit. Our economy is barely improving in spite of huge government spending programs. Bigness (in government) has always turned out badly. The current purpose (guardian of the people) of American government is failing.

Isn't it time to return America to the values that made it great?

INTRODUCTION

Capitalistic Greed – Good or Bad?

Greed is listed as one on the seven deadly sins. All religions and every religious society stigmatizes greed. The Wikipedia definition of greed is "the inordinate desire to possess wealth, goods, or objects of abstract value with the intention to keep it for one's self, far beyond the dictates of basic survival and comfort. It is applied to a markedly high desire for and pursuit of wealth, status, and power". The capitalistic economic system is often derided as a greed inspired system.

If the definition of greed was applied to civilization today and its ancestry, most achievers would be classified as greedy as they possess wealth far beyond that which is needed for survival and comfort. However, the label of greedy has never appeared in history books to describe the kings, the aristocracy, the conquerors, or other members of the elite class. And, I don't believe the label was used in print or conversation during the lifetimes of those individuals! It seems the label was more relevant for the merchants of those periods who wanted to achieve greater wealth and become part of the upper class. The merchant class following the dark ages was responsible for the increased standard of living in Western Europe. Merchants introduced Europe to a vast variety of different goods and methods of production. In the process, instead of being respected for their contribution, many were seen as greedy unscrupulous businessmen. The large profit from managing their businesses properly was seen as a result of gouging by the other members of society.

Although the aristocracy did nothing to enhance the livelihood of their constituency, these leeches somehow escaped the greedy label. The aristocracy's main concern was maintaining appearances not actively pursuing (like the merchant class) business dealings to increase their wealth by creating a better, more varied productive life for their subjects. Kings were mostly concerned with increasing their reputation for their legacy. They strived for more glory by conquest. They needed more wealth to do this. Either they taxed their citizens for the funds to war or they sent out armies to conquer and plunder (ex. – their action after the discovery of the new world). Business ventures were too common and beneath them.

The pursuit of wealth (or a better life) is the most basic of human desires. Yet, in the circumstance of greed, it becomes a demeaning behavior. The negative connotation of greed comes from the religious (or spiritual) concept that all men must be their brother's keeper (If the action of one man deprives the other of the essentials for living, it is immoral). Therefore if greedy action causes damage to others, it is often characterized as unjustified and immoral. Because the degree of damage (and the type of damage) is so vague, it is easy to vilify the achiever (if an enemy) without just cause. Wealthy merchants in feudal times were a threat to the aristocracy, so propaganda about their greed was useful in controlling their influence in society. A merchant who was labeled greedy by the aristocracy often became a social outcast and suffered in his business enterprise.

Propaganda that incited jealousy and outrage by the masses has been a political tool used to gain power and deflect criticism since the beginning of the human race. And, it is no different today. The focus of propaganda today is on greed. In order to gain power, American politicians are inciting the masses to vote for wealth equalization. This is a call to undo the consequences of greed ('to keep wealth far beyond the dictates of survival or comfort'). And, this is the antitheses of the American Dream since it restricts dreamers to be limited in the scope of their dream. The negative aspect of greed has been reduced to having more (how much is unspecified) than your fellow citizens which causes damage because it provides holders and their offspring an unfair advantage in access to current goods and services (ex. – healthcare) and future achievement. The American concept that hard work deserves superior rewards is challenged by this propaganda redefining the limits to which greed applies.

Although the concept of greed hasn't changed since the socialization of man, the circumstances to which it is applied has changed dramatically in most countries of the world. As man's standard of living has risen dramatically in these countries, the greedy action of individuals no longer threatens the lives of other members of society. Instead, it is perceived to degrade the quality of life of the less fortunate. In America, the greedy (the new American definition - those unwilling to pay their fair share in taxes) are responsible for stratifying social and economic mobility (the oppression of the underprivileged prevents them from becoming part of the lower or middle class). This stratification prevents the less fortunate from acquiring all the benefits of home ownership, good education, good entertainment, a nice retirement plan, good healthcare, and a sense of self-worth. This is a far cry from the consequences attributed to greed in the Industrial Revolution and ancient society. Starvation, disease, and squalorous living conditions were the responsibility of the greedy then.

Many socialists attribute society's vast change in living conditions to the average worker. Yet, since the fall of the Roman Empire, nothing that the average worker did really improved the standard of living. In fact, nothing that anyone did changed general living conditions. Commerce virtually stopped as its cost vastly increased as safety vanished. And, similar security issues created a feudal system where land ownership became stratified in the fiefdoms. Greed was restricted to the lords who wanted more power. Rewards of wealth and upward mobility to the common man were available mainly to those who could improve the fighting machine.

Not until the plague in the middle of the 14th century (wiping out 1/3 of the population) did circumstances change. Land ownership and higher wage opportunities for half the remaining population opened up. And, the standard of living of the worker significantly increased. The merchant class became vastly expanded after this period as worker wages rose along with per/capita demand for the merchants' products. The merchant class was not composed of the average working man. They were entrepreneurs willing to take substantial risk to life and capital unlike the average risk-adverse man. The greed (wanting to live much better than others) of the entrepreneur propelled him to take the risk necessary to achieve the un-ordinary (opening up new markets and new businesses). And, he did.

It took another 400 years before the arrival of the Industrial Revolution. Again, it was not the average man that dreamed up all the inventions that eventually led to the modern world and living conditions unthinkable in earlier times. It was individuals willing to take the risk of failure (failure likely led to extreme poverty and social ostracization) that propelled society's advancement. The inducement of living a kingly life then was the incentive driving economic improvement in efficiency (It is important to note that the massively successful entrepreneur, likely to be classified as greedy, was preceded by hundreds of thousands of entrepreneurial failures. This risk taken by the entrepreneur is drastically underestimated by those who see only greed in the successful.).

Entrepreneurs, risk takers who wanted much more than the ordinary man (definition of greedy men), have been responsible for the incredible life style even the poor enjoy today (they live better than the Kings of the 19th century!) in the Western world. For this reason, entreprenurial greed must be considered good! What type of greed is bad? When economic production is stagnant (assuming a constant population), then any change in its distribution will result in less for some. Greed would be harmful to those getting less. The political systems that fear change and thus do not promote risk taking have been shown to have stagnant (at best) economies. The leaders of these political systems (aristocracies, dictatorships, religious orders, extreme socialism – communism) always want and take the best for themselves. These systems promote the harmful greed that is so detrimental to society. The fact that an individual possesses more due to his efforts that have bettered the living conditions of countless other members of society should not lead to his characterization as greedy (regardless of how much he wants to keep in his lifetime). Instead, the label should be attributed to those who attempt to benefit themselves at the expense of society. These individuals should be easy to identify by following the trail of their propaganda which is espoused only for self-benefit.

CHAPTER 1

The Day America Died - 11/04/2012
(A Likely Future Narrative)

After 250 years of unfettered freedom, the country whose economic and moral lighthouse drew millions of repressed men and women from all corners of the world was infected with the fatal human virus of jealousy along with the hatred accompanied by it. The American population became pitted against each other as the rhetoric of the United States President hammered on the unfairness of the gap between the rich and the poor. A President who had won his first term in office as the man who would bring the country together and solve its economic problems by working with all Americans with compromise and understanding had changed his colors soon after being elected to office. Compromise was viewed by this President as a migration of opposite views to accept his political and social agenda. From the first day of his virginal campaign, he knew the promise he made of bringing harmony to his country was a lie. President Obama was a communist. His political viewpoint was so far left that it could only lead to divisiveness in a country founded on individual independence. Obama's charisma and his false promise carried the 2008 elections for him and his party. The beginning of America's death march had started.

CHAPTER 1

Although President Obama and his party had won total control of the government with majority party representation in both the House and the Senate, he discovered that there was still significant opposition to the socialistic policies he wished to initiate. Many Democratic legislators were old school. They still believed in the principles of independence and freedom sanctioned by America's forefathers. And, many Americans, shocked to learn that their President would actually try to legislate far leftist programs, united to form the Tea Party to oppose the President's agenda. The combination of conservative Democrats and the new power of the Tea Party prevented the President from pushing many of his ideas onto the American people. Then, the 2010 Congressional elections shifted power away from the Democrats as the Conservative Republicans won a large majority in the House. The Democratic platform of harmony and compromise formulated by President Obama had stopped working. A new platform had to be created for the 2012 election. If harmony and compromise wasn't working, then the opposite philosophy, division and blame was a likely candidate. And, that is precisely the platform chosen by the President and his party. The campaign of what was wrong with America started. And, the blame platform took root.

It was time to blame the Republican Party for everything. The Democratic attack stated that Republican policies starting under President George Bush had caused the terrible recession, the repression of human rights internationally through war, the repression of the domestic human rights of women, of racial minorities, of sexual minorities, and of religious minorities. The Republican policies were also to blame for global warming, for attacking the rights of illegal immigrants, and for the unfair wealth gap between the rich and the poor. The most damning accusation however was to blame the Republicans for creating an unequal playing field where many underprivileged Americans could never achieve their dreams. Republicans were to be blamed for ending the 'American Dream'! The Democratic platform was to portray the Republicans as the party of the establishment and the rich while portraying their own party as the party of the people and the poor. Karl Marx's ideology and philosophy had been exhumed! And, amazingly after 100 years of failure in communistic Russia and China, the majority of Americans decided these ideas had credibility. President Obama was re-elected.

That brought Americans to December 2012 and the Fiscal Cliff. The battle being fought between the Republicans and the Democrats was supposedly over whether tax rates should be raised on the rich. The Republican position was that raising rates on the rich in desperate economic times would send the economy spiraling downward. The Democrat position was that raising rates on the rich was only fair and wouldn't be detrimental to the economy. The Fiscal Cliff was legislation put into effect as a compromise to extend the Bush Administration's tax cuts while also expanding the debt ceiling in 2011. Republicans wanted to extend the Bush program of lower taxes while the Democrats wanted to expand government spending programs.

CHAPTER 1

A compromise was reached which stated that the Bush tax cuts would end and certain government spending programs would be curtailed on December 31, 2012 if some other compromise couldn't be reached before then. The 2011 compromise began being labeled as the Fiscal Cliff in 2012 as the political parties became more entrenched in their positions and the looming drastic increase in taxes and reduction in government spending appeared likely to send the economy into a severe tailspin and was likened to falling off a cliff. With both parties acknowledging the terrible consequences to the American economy and people of not reaching a compromise, the expectation was that these politicians would come to their senses and hammer out an agreement.

Unfortunately, that did not happen. Republicans were willing to move to raise tax revenue if the Democrats would agree to accept significant cuts in entitlement programs. The Republican position was that with federal debt at 100% of GDP, any future debt expansion as a percentage of the GDP would result in future economic catastrophe. And, as the annual federal deficit was growing faster than GDP, action needed to be taken to change this outcome. As an increase in taxation on the rich would only accomplish an extremely small part of the needed reduction, major cuts in government spending also needed to occur. The Democratic position was that the injustice of the rich not paying their fair share was the main problem that needed to be addressed and that government debt as a percentage of the GDP was not a pressing problem. With the Republican belief that without spending cuts, the economy would be doomed in the future and the

Democratic view that rectifying the injustice of the tax system was extremely important, only a minor compromise was reached. The Republicans agreed to a tax increase on the rich (those making over $250,000) but only compromised to delay spending cuts until March 2013. Sequestration was the label used to describe the automatic spending cuts that would take place if a new budget wasn't agreed upon by the Congress and President.

The Fiscal cliff was averted by two months and replaced by sequestration as Republicans caved to allow tax increases. However, the Democrats failed to achieve their goal of raising the debt ceiling in this period and the impending crisis was pushed to October 2013 when government funding could no longer be authorized as the ceiling came into play. After many political charades and gamesmanship, on October 17, both parties agreed to the Continuing Appropriations Act, 2014. However, the debt ceiling issue was again pushed down the road (to February 2014).

Republicans, however, changed their political strategy in December 2013 when major problems with Obamacare became apparent. Instead of being steadfast supporters of fiscal responsibility bearing the title (according to the liberal press) of uncooperative obstructionists, Republican leaders chose to become more cooperative and approved a two year budget which eliminated sequestration. Republicans hoped that the problems with Obamacare would push enough voters into the Republican camp to win the 2014 elections. Although the Republican leadership in December hadn't caved on increasing the debt ceiling, that would happen in February 2014. The Republicans wanted the public to focus solely on the failures of Obamacare. They put their conservative principles on the back burner in hopes of resurrecting them after their expected win in the 2014 elections. The Democratic tactic of no compromise had led to a Republican capitulation of their principles.

Well before October 2013, the Democrats had decided to adopt this no compromise tactic. GDP figures showed the economy starting to improve at the end of 2012. QE 3 was put in place in September 2012 with the Fed buying $40B/month in bank mortgages and another $45B/month in other assets. This asset buying program unleashed a huge investor demand for real-estate. And, housing prices started to climb in October of 2012. By April, in previously depressed areas such as California they climbed as much as 30%. With home values rising, consumers started to increase their spending and the economy picked up. With the economy rising and the deficit declining (from decreased spending and increased tax revenues), the Democrats could posture their economic program was working.

In budget negotiations, the Democrats claimed the Republicans were obstructionists and bent on destroying America's social safety net. President Obama claimed that because his economic policies were working, he should be allowed to increase social spending above sequestration levels. And, as the recent increased taxation on the rich was not depressing the economy, it showed further taxation of the wealthy would not be a bad thing! The Democrats had adopted the tactic that they would offer very little in compromise to the Republicans in any budget negotiations. They would make it impossible for Republicans to gain any major concessions. And, the Democrats would either get what they wanted (massively increased spending and higher taxes on the rich) or they would allow a government shutdown to take place and blame the Republicans for allowing it to happen. In either case, Democrats felt the Republicans were in a no-win situation. If they gave up their fiscal conservative principles by accepting the unconditional demands of the Democrats, they would lose many conservative voters. Or, if they refused to vote for a fiscal ball-breaker budget, they would have to shut the government down. In either case, the Democrats believed that they had the Republicans in a vise (and many Republican politicians believed it also)!

Democrats knew the most probable choice for the Republicans was to continue to negotiate for conservative principles up until a government shutdown was imminent and then have both parties agree to kick the can down the road. Neither party would then be blamed for an actual shutdown. But the Democrats, in control of the liberal press, could politicize each circumstance of brinkmanship as Republican irresponsibility and unwillingness to compromise. The Democratic Party and its President fully embraced the concept of creating multiple crises to gain increased political power!

This Democratic strategy had pressured the Republicans into choosing the fatal political strategy of sacrificing (conservative) principles. The Republican abandonment of the principles of conservative financial responsibility ensured the Democrats of a win in the 2014 elections. The Fiscal Cliff and the ensuing debt ceiling crisis, instead of forcing the political parties to act in the best interest of the American people, became the vehicle the Democrats would use to put themselves back in total political power. The unwillingness on the part of President Obama to concede any point in his political agenda was instrumental in the Democratic win. So, although the official propaganda of the President and his Party spoke to working together and compromise, the opposite had propelled the Democrats to win full control of the government.

Obama's goal was achieved with the ideology that the ends justified the means. If the public had to suffer from crisis to crisis so that he and his Party would have total control of the government in 2014, this was the outcome he cherished. He knew if the government was shut down and the economy unraveled as a result, the public would demand more government intervention and government assistance. A bigger more controlling government fit exactly into his plans to turn America into a socialistic country. If the Republicans caved on his demands, he could also transform America immediately by instituting more socialistic programs. And if each crisis could be blamed on the Republicans, his Party would win Congressional control and then transform the economy in the last two years of his term. An economy in turmoil or a political whirlwind was exactly what he needed to achieve his political aspirations. President Obama had laid out his political philosophy in the 2012 election (no compromise, scorch political opponents, and turn the country to radical socialism) and had followed it to the tee.

In 2014, as voters elected Democrats to hold the majority of seats in Congress, power was passed to the socialists. 250 years of individual independence was dead along with its associated individual liberties. In the following years, societal equity would exist in the same form as in communist Russia and China in the 20th century. Finally, all society lived equally at the lowest common standard of living except those politically elite who controlled the favors of the government. America, the shining beacon of liberty and opportunity, had been suffocated by the theme of equality of outcomes. President Obama had realized the Dreams of his Father. November 4, 2012 was the day America died.

CHAPTER 2

A Dream Ended

Chapter 1 of this book describes a likely scenario for America. 4,000 years of human history shows individual freedoms being dominated by government control. Few societies were democratic and based on the rights of the individual. And, in the blink of an eye, those societies vanished! 99% of humans have lived under the whims of the other 1% (the kings, the emperors, the pharaohs, the dictators, and the dominating political and religious regimes). The explanation for this phenomena is simple.

Groups of people gravitate to the charisma of a leader. And, 95%+ of the population would rather be a follower than a leader. Most people either think they are incapable of leading, don't want the responsibility in leading, don't want to listen to the public criticism of their decisions, or don't want to be in the public eye. Most people want to do what's comfortable for themselves. And, politics doesn't fit the bill. These characteristics of the population can easily be seen in all aspects of society but stand out in educational classrooms. The average student doesn't want to be singled out because of the embarrassment that this situation might warrant. The student much prefers to be anonymous and not called upon for his opinion. And if called upon, in seeking leadership (teacher) approval, the student will try to please the teacher by regurgitating what he has been told. Because 95% of the population's comfort zone is as a follower, this leaves 5% to compete to become the leaders who make the rules. As children, we all learned that the person making the rules for any game was in a very powerful position to win. Adjusting the rules to benefit the rule maker usually leads to a large unfair advantage. In the political arena, that's the attraction of becoming a politician! However, in order to be successful in gaining the acceptance of the population (vs. the competition), this individual must convince the majority that his rule making ability will benefit them more than the opponent's. As the general population would much rather hear how things will get better versus a less appealing diagnosis, all successful politicians will lie about what's possible in order to become a leader (or part of the leadership establishment). Once a leadership position has been obtained, the politician will work on consolidating his power by creating alliances with other politicians. Depending on the political structure that exists, this process can lead to total power. If the political system allows the allocation of money and the control of the army and the police to be under the power of the premier politician, then total power will eventually reside in the premier leader. And, total power has always lead to the subjugation of the masses. The goal of politicians is to achieve this ultimate power.

America's forefathers recognized that powerful governments regularly dominated their citizens with laws passed by a small group of elite power holders. Since they cherished freedom, they attempted to create a governmental structure that would never be able to consolidate enough power in a small group of men or entities that could undermine the rights of its citizens. Church (the second most powerful organization at the time) and State were mandated to be separate. Three branches of government, the judicial, the legislative, and the executive were given different powers. And, the ability of the government to confiscate currency, land, or other resources of the individual was limited. Also, the ability of the government to make laws controlling peoples' rights was limited. The control of governmental power and corresponding rights of the people were prescribed in the Constitution and the Bill of Rights.

Today, America's freedoms are on the ropes. Two political parties over the past 80 years have slowly been usurping political and economic power by instituting laws that have vastly increased the size and scope of the U.S. federal and state governments. The magnitude of the power grab is easily seen in the massive growth in government spending in relation to private spending. In 1930, total government spending as a percentage of GDP was around 13%. Today, total government spending as a percentage of GDP is around 37%. Two parties now control the disposition of 37% of wealth in America. These parties make our laws and attempt to control our thoughts through main stream media. Americans have forfeited many of their liberties in response to Republican and Democratic lies about how the government is best at caring for its citizens. Our forefathers would have been aghast to think this could ever happen.

CHAPTER 3

America on the Ropes

The temperature of the world is rising both physically and politically. Global warming is not the only subject of fear in the wealthy developed world. Joblessness is rising in the rich countries and the threat of less to the majority of these populations is becoming an increasingly alarming concern.

There is an indisputable connection between 'global warming' and unemployment. That connection is politics! The citizens of wealthy countries are being played by their elected officials who pay homage, not to the electorate but to the political party responsible for their election. Global warming is a 100,000 year cyclical climate condition (see chart on page 33) that has been used by politicians to increase their control over society by justifying the creation of more rules and regulations.

Global warming is the latest political power grabbing ploy in a long line of issues used to enhance political power. Free trade was the prior issue. Free trade is the cause of unemployment in the developed world. It has been relentlessly promoted by politicians everywhere. Free trade has resulted in the biggest increase in the divide between the rich and poor in recent times (Trade arbitraging slave labor wages has created huge profits for multi-national corporations. These profits have vastly benefited the elite business executive class, as rising stock prices tied to earnings created massive stock option profits for these executives. And, executive total compensation has become hundreds and thousands of times that of the average worker). Politicians are now using this division to increase their power by creating more rules and regulations to redistribute wealth.

Politics has always been the game of enhancing the power of the elite political players. Where historically they were the kings, the emperors, the dictators, or the religious leaders, today in America they are the Democratic and Republican Parties' political leaders. Amazingly, throughout history, small groups lead by charismatic leaders have always been able to dominate and gain control over the overwhelming majority. And, in the process, these leaders and their close conspirators provided a godly lifestyle for themselves and their offspring regardless of the subjugation they required of their constituency.

The western world, after casting away the shackles of its kings, is on its way to re-enter the subservient world run by political rulers. America led the western world's people to freedom. The country is still the main hope to carry their founders' liberty vision into the future. Will Americans cherish their heritage of freedom or follow the lead of all historic societies and sink into the servitude of the political lords? It's time to discuss how recent events have played into the hands of politicians and how Americans are being affected.

AMERICA ON THE ROPES

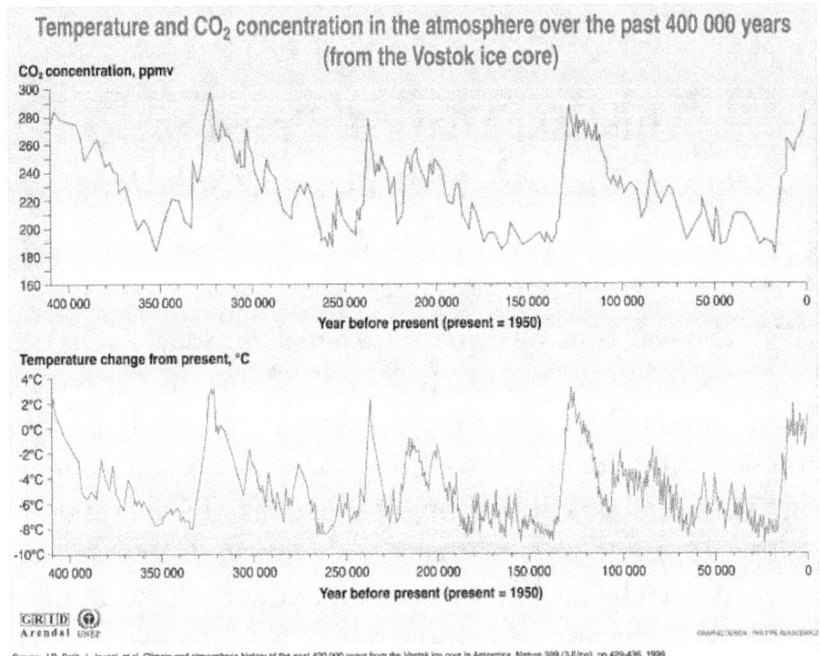

Temperature and CO₂ concentration in the atmosphere over the past 400 000 years (from the Vostok ice core)

Source: J.R. Petit, J. Jouzel, et al. Climate and atmospheric history of the past 420 000 years from the Vostok ice core in Antarctica, Nature 399 (3/June), pp 429-436, 1999.

The source of this graph is UNEP/GRID-Arendal and its web address is:
http://www.grida.no/graphicslib/detail/temperature-and-co2-concentration-in-the-atmosphere-over-the-past-400-000-years_1561

The cartographer/designer is Phillippe Rekacewicz, UNEP/GRID-Arendal

---

The top graph shows CO2 concentration in the atmosphere; the bottom one shows average temperature departure from the 1950 value. Two observations are quite apparent:

- For the last 400,000 years at least, the average temperature was significantly colder than today.

- Wild temperature fluctuations were common before any possible impact of human civilizations. Mankind was not responsible for the temperature spikes that occurred at almost every 100,000 year interval prior to civilization.

CHAPTER 4

The Last Years of Freedom
(Recent History – Problems and Solutions)

The year 2000 was forecast to be a doomsday year by the pessimists. On the astrological side, every year resulting in three zeros had massive astrological negative implications. On the more rational side, there was a technology issue that was feared might cause massive disruptions to the electronic systems that ran the world. Computer usage had risen by 2000 to the point that the world economies would be devastated if their operation was defective.

In the early days of task development in computer programming, memory space was extremely costly. Programs were written with only 2 digits instead of 4 to describe the year portion of the date to be in memory. Many experts in the technology community worried that old computers and old computer chips with the date flaw that ran various important and necessary automated systems would either shut down, lose data, overwrite old data, or just go haywire. Any operation that lost even a small portion of data would be devastated. Imagine a bank having 10,000,000 customers and losing information on 1,000. How would it balance its books?

Luckily or by good management, the world sailed through 2000. Times were good. Interest rates were low as the Fed had prepped them since 1998 for the worst outcome of the technology memory glitch. The real estate market was going crazy with low interest rates. The financial markets were booming with the internet phenomenon and low interest rates. And, the developing former communist countries' economies were exploding by supplying cheap goods to the Western World. Wages everywhere were going up, and all assets classes were on the rise. Everyone felt the world was a better place and the economy and wages would continue to improve. In early 2001 economic events smashed this outlook.

Cheap money and optimism had driven consumers to enjoy life. And, they were willing to maximize the experience through borrowing. Wages were expected to continue rising and therefore make the debt affordable. Unfortunately, that expectation was wrong. These consumers had driven economic growth through their spending and in the process had raised business expectations about future growth. The corresponding growth in investment to meet future business expectations along with debt spending by the consumer led to massive overspending.

When the Fed decided the party was excessive and raised rates, demand slowed and the business community suffered a severe blow. With profits radically declining and companies having significant overcapacity, the business community hunkered down. They cut staff, put a freeze on wages, and went looking for a cheaper place to do business. When the Fed saw the economy in free fall, they immediately reversed their earlier stance on raising rates and immediately started cutting rates.

Then came 9/11/2001. Although there was an initial shock to the economic system, the government's reaction was to massively increase spending while continuing to lower interest rates. Although business was slow to respond in the way of hiring because of overcapacity and the near deathblow they had just suffered, the consumer somehow continued spending and borrowing. With low interest rates, the consumers real estate holdings (his house), the main staple of his wealth, reversed its minor drop in 2001 and started rising dramatically.

As the consumers' core wealth increased, consumers felt they could continue to borrow to maintain their standard of living. The construction industry and the financial industry boomed and carried the economy with it, reversing the 2001-2003 recession. Businesses however kept wages constrained. Overall, the wage earner was not holding his own. To compensate, the consumer borrowed and increased their purchases of cheap foreign goods. As long as the housing bubble propelled consumers wealth and the economy, the consumer could continue to spend to maintain the standard of living they were accustomed to. Unfortunately, that ended in 2008.

Real estate prices had boomed for almost 14 years with only a mild drop in 2001. It was perceived that prices could only go higher. This belief had propelled most financial institutions to reduce their standards for borrowing to almost nothing. Loans were made with almost no down payment to almost anyone who could pay a loan application fee. The banks and other lending institutions had seen their profits rise with initial high fees for mortgage applications and also home loan applications. They were more concerned with keeping this stream of revenue than with the risk associated with the long-term viability of the borrower.

As the ratio of risky loans to high quality loans grew on the balance sheets of these institutions, the likelihood of more defaults grew. Also, as many of these loans were short-term and had a variable interest rate structure, rising interest rates increased the future risk of default. After 9/11/2001, the Fed had cut rates to almost zero. Once the economy started to recover in 2003, the Fed started its policy of raising rates which lasted through 2007. The inevitable started to happen in 2007 when the default rate started to rise. The higher default rate put pressure on rising housing prices. The real estate bubble had stalled and was about to crash. Once prices stopped going higher, institutions, individuals, and speculators started worrying about their risk exposure in real estate. Real estate needed no longer to be bought but to be sold. The upward momentum turned around and the Bubble burst.

Housing prices had reached unsustainable levels and economics took over. Trillions of dollars had been bet by the consumer, by the financial institutions, and by the Government through Freddie Mac and Fannie Mae backed loans. This bet was lost. The U.S. consumer who had borrowed beyond his means for over 10 years and the financial institutions who had lent to him were in massive trouble.

The U.S. economy, with 70% of GDP dependent on consumer spending, was on the precipice of a Great Depression. Instead of allowing the chips to fall as they may, the Government decided again a massive spending program was needed to avert the suffering and unknown disruption that would be caused by a bankrupt financial system. The Great Depression had led to 20 years of hardship. No one wanted this to happen again. So, the government again turned on the monetary printing presses and at the same time massively increased spending programs. (In 1999, federal and state expenditures accounted for 33% of US GDP. In 2011, after two massive spending programs, government expenditures represented 41% of GDP. Government spending increased by $3.1 trillion dollars in these 12 years while GDP increased $5.7 trillion. Government spending was responsible for over 50% of GDP growth! Since 2008, Government spending has increased $.175 trillion/yr. while GDP has increased by $.263 trillion/yr.!!). The last 4 years of government spending have represented 66% of the growth in GDP.

The U.S. is now in its 5th year of trying to regain economic footing. Government spending has allowed GDP growth to stay positive although unemployment has been slow to respond. However, the current level of government spending is now so high that there is question as to how long it is sustainable and whether the short-term benefits will offset the long-term consequences. As the government does not produce tangible goods or new consumer services, the only benefit of high government spending might be that it will stimulate private sector production. The government's bet is that by propping up consumer income through government payments and by inducing businesses to invest though low interest rates, economic growth will take hold and return the economy to average growth. Will that bet be successful?

THE LAST YEARS OF FREEDOM

In the past 12 years, America's elected representatives have instituted more safety nets to minimize the suffering of the unfortunate. By doing so, they have made the government much more powerful under the premise that politicians can solve social problems better than private industry. It's time to evaluate that premise.

DISCUSSION POINT 1
Government Support Programs - Are They Effective?

The economy needs to produce jobs in order to grow. Small businesses have produced 70% of new job growth in the U.S. for the past 20 years. People starting these businesses have been the most productive workers in the country. The success of small business comes from necessity, risk taking, hard work and imagination and little organizational bureaucracy. If the small business owner fails, he most likely will lose everything he has. Therefore, he will work harder, make adjustments to his product, and always be trying to understand the market for his product. These traits of successful entrepreneurs give them the edge they need in order to successfully compete with big business. As the small business entrepreneur has been the instrument of past job growth in the U.S., it is logical that government policy should promote incentives for the small businessman in order to achieve job growth. However, current government policies have added burdens to small businesses not incentives.

The most expensive of these newly instituted policies is Obamacare. Obama's health care policy is costing all businesses higher health care costs. The necessity of complying with the myriad of regulations requires employers to add costly additional resources. Additional employees are need-ed and must be paid to understand and administer health-care programs according to the law. As a percentage of costs, the small business owner will incur a much higher incre-mental cost than the large corporations to comply with the new healthcare laws.

Next, the new regulatory laws on lending will also make it more costly to borrow from the banks. Bank costs go up with regulation and these costs get passed through to the borrower. Since small businesses are perceived to be more risky than big businesses and are more reliant on expan-sion loans, small businesses will be more affected than large corporations by the new financial regulatory rules that are aimed at reducing bank risk.

Another anti-business policy is Obama's program that in-creases taxes on the rich. This also has implications for the small business owner. Obama's definition of rich is someone making over $250K/year. In the case of the small business owner, there are numerous problems with using this sim-plistic number. On the business capital side, the smallest of small business owners have to have invested at least $250K in their business to attain any chance of success. As mentioned earlier, this capital is subject to loss at any moment. The risk associated with investing in your own business is the highest possible risk in the investing world. If your business fails, not only do you lose most of your capital, but you also lose your job. The small business owner has the most concentrated risk of any investor. Because most small business owners usually do not have significant excess capital, any hiccup in operations, can result in a total loss of the business. And, if the business environment changes, one year's $250K gain may turn into a loss the next year. Additional taxes on small businesses just decreases the margin for error that could lead to failure. As this government's tax plan does not take into count the risk factors associated with small businesses, the plan to simply add a higher tax to anyone making over $250K/year is likely to have a significant negative effect on small businesses.

The newly instituted healthcare and financial regulatory policies, in addition to a higher taxes on the wealthy are very negative policies in regard to small business. They are also having a negative impact on job creation. The government's newly instituted regulations and increased taxes haven't resolved the economic crisis. Since politicians have also been responsible for the current extremely low interest rates, that policy needs also to be evaluated.

Has the policy of low interest rates promoted by the government worked? There is no question that financial institutions and large corporations have benefited greatly by this policy. Financial institutions are making billions by borrowing at ¼% and lending to foreign sovereign nations and large AAA rated corporations at significantly higher rates. These large corporations are using these loans to either buy back their own stock or bonds or to invest in new plant and equipment in the developing world where returns of 20%+ are common. Unfortunately, the low interest rates have not led to domestic investment. The consumer has benefited somewhat on large purchases where the producing company passes on a low rate to the consumer. (However, credit card rates have not come down with the Fed's lower rate.) The consumer has also benefited by the fact that low interest rates have created a positive environment for his holdings of stock and debt assets. They have risen substantially. The positive benefit of this rise in asset classes has been offset by a higher inflation rate (caused by a rise in the price of commodities - the commodity asset class) and also by the decrease in the income of holders of money market funds and other short-term financial instruments such as U.S. Treasuries.

Many of the holders of these instruments are older middle to upper class workers who have either retired or were shortly planning to retire. Instead of having a nest egg that would have been returned a historic 4% to 5% on riskless short-term financial instruments, these individuals are looking now at receiving ¼% on their nest eggs. The retirement plans for these folks have been scrambled! With trillions of dollars of retirement investments, a 4% yearly reduction amounts to hundreds of billions that are now out of the pockets of the older consumers and savers. In addition, without these yearly funds to count on in retirement, these older consumers must cut back on current spending and save more for retirement.

Low interest rates have caused older Americans to earn much less income while allowing financial institutions to earn more, and allowing large corporations to earn more by investing in the developing world. It appears that the government's low interest rate policy has resulted in baby boomer retirement plans subsidizing the large institutions and their investment in the developing world. Although low interest rates have stimulated investment and jobs, unfortunately that investment and job creation is happening almost solely outside the U.S. Although there has been a positive wealth effect from this low interest rate policy, it's hard to believe that higher stock and bond prices offset the negatives of lower investment income and worries of retirement security. No current job growth and the current economic job outlook reinforces the truth of this observation. The low interest rate policy promoted by our elected officials has been a failure.

The last major government program intended to right the economy include the Government policies of extending benefit payments to the unemployed, reducing payroll taxes, not increasing personal income taxes, and bank and corporate bailout programs. These policies have forestalled the onset of another Great Depression. However, the lack of job creation, the high jobless rate and the low confidence level as shown in recent polls still leaves much doubt as to whether these spending programs will have a positive lasting effect.

Political (government) management of the economy hasn't worked yet even as total government debt has expanded to dangerously high levels. And, as the wealth divide between the rich and poor is at the highest level of the past 80 years, political social policy hasn't worked either. The fact that small businesses have created 70% of American jobs in the last 20 years would indicate that it is private industry that should be relied upon to resolve the current economic crisis, not the politicians fiddling with ineffective government programs!

DISCUSSION POINT 2 -
Big Business' Response to Government Stimulus

In the past, the Federal Reserve managed to stimulate growth with low interest rates as did increased government spending. Why hasn't that policy produced greater results for the economy the last 4 years? Why hasn't there been more job creation and U.S. investment in plant and equipment with current government policies? The answers to these questions can be found in consumer and business perceptions. Since recovery in most recessions starts with increased business investment, a good question to be asked first is why hasn't there been more investment in the U.S.?

The answer is simple. U.S. businesses are uncompetitive with those of China and the other developing nations. Wages in the U.S. are at least 5 times higher than in those other countries. Also, U.S. businesses face major regulatory hurdles that severely increase costs and the risk of doing business. These hurdles include healthcare, discrimination, environmental, and human management resource issues among other expensive regulatory rules that require compliance. Many of these rules do not exist in developing countries. Because the cost of doing business overseas is much less expensive, profit margins are usually higher and companies can earn more on their investments abroad. Returns have been so attractive in these developing countries that U.S. corporations have invested trillions of dollars there in the last 15 years. And, future growth in the developing countries also has been and is projected to be much higher than that of the U.S. Therefore foreign investment has attracted most long-term investment dollars.

The higher projected returns of investing overseas have cannibalized investment in the U.S. Low interest rates and easy money in the U.S. has led to the financing of the developed countries, not to business building in the U.S. Also, a large portion of investment dollars going overseas are to businesses that export to the U.S. consumer market. The consumer market in the developing countries usually represents only 30% of their economies vs. 70% in the U.S. markets. The greatest overseas opportunity is the biggest market, the export market. This added competition has been an increasing burden on the U.S. economy.

In regard to the consumer, as business opportunities in the U.S. have been stifled, so therefore have job opportunities and wages. The consumer's spending power comes from their wages, their investment income, and from their core wealth perception. The job market is poor, wages are being constrained by foreign competition, low interest rates are reducing investment income and retirement security, and personal wealth is being restrained by weak home prices. The largest group of consumers and savers in the U.S. are the baby boomers. They had expectations of retiring comfortably when interest on their retirement accounts was paying 5%. Now with similar interest rates at .25%, they need to cut back on their current spending in order to possibly still have enough money for a feasible retirement. Reduction in the interest received in the baby boomers' retirement accounts has reduced this group of consumer income by hundreds of billions of dollars. How can the consumer in this situation drive demand to lead to economic growth? They can't.

To sum up, the reason government policies that worked in the past to stimulate the economy are not working today is that the economic environment has changed. Never before has the magnitude of business competition between domestic U.S. companies and companies in the developing world been so great. The release of close to a billion workers from communism has resulted in a tidal wave of cheap labor and cheap working environments that have overwhelmed the U.S. and also the rest of the Western World!

Government programs have forestalled a possible Great Depression by increasing the government's debt by close to $4.9 trillion dollars over the past 4 years. Using an average of $1.22 trillion, this excess debt spending represents about 8% of yearly GDP. U.S. GDP growth last year was less than 2%. Without excess government spending, the economy would have declined over 6% (a depression indeed)! Although a possible depression has been averted, 4 years later deficit spending is still around 7% of GDP. And, since the government doesn't produce consumable products, a government spending deficit higher than the growth rate of the economy means less goods and services are actually being produced. The economy is in a disguised serious recession which shows the policies of our elected officials are failing. Why do they insist on continuing down the same path?

DISCUSSION POINT 3
The Seeds of American Problems -
Financial Crisis or Free Trade?

Most governmental officials, politicians, economists and business pundits have laid the blame of this recession on the bursting of the real-estate bubble and the resulting financial crisis, not on foreign competition. Their opinion would indicate a belief that real-estate speculation was the only reason the U.S. is its current economic situation. And, without the bubble, the U.S. wouldn't be in trouble.

This analysis has led to the current faulty economic policies attempting to get the economy back on track. The Democrats and the Fed have proposed more quantitative (printing money) easing. The Republicans have proposed lower taxes and less government spending to achieve a greater trickle-down effect. Both these plans ignore that with overseas investment returns of 20%+ vs. domestic investments returns of less than 5%, neither will work. The Republican plan will not provide enough business incentives to narrow the return differential to make domestic investment attractive. And, therefore it will not create jobs. And, the Democratic plan of cheap money will only lead to more investment overseas.

The standard of living is so much lower in the developing world that the developed economies can't compete. Corporations in the developed world have invested trillions of dollars in the developing world because the returns and expected returns are much higher than in the U.S. (and also much higher than in Western Europe). The developing world has a huge competitive advantage that is being exploited by big business. The current economic policies are only adding to the problem. The policy of globalization is working to transfer wealth from the developed countries to the developing countries.

Our previous discussion showed that current policies are not stimulating either new domestic investment or consumer spending. If the economy was simply in disequilibrium because of the real-estate bubble bust, then our economic problems would have already been solved by traditional means. However, world economic disequilibrium is being caused by the loss of competitiveness of the Western World. America's free trade policy that allows slave labor to replace middle class labor has sown the seeds of the economic malaise in our country.

DISCUSSION POINT 4
Free Trade – Theory, Practice, and Problems

Free trade has been promoted as a significant driver for domestic and world growth by most politicians and economists. And many elite intellectuals attribute the Great Depression to anti-trade government policies in the 1930s. However, trade restrictions at that time only involved members of the developed countries. Although the disparity of living standards was as great as it is today between the developed and underdeveloped world, there were no developing countries competing in the same markets as existed in the developed world. Therefore low wages in the developing world had no influence on wages in developed countries. Trade policies concerning the underdeveloped world were not an issue.

The standard of living, in 1930, of the middle classes of the countries in the developed world were very comparable. Wage equilibrium was not an issue at the time. When trade protectionism policies were instituted by the developed countries, the export and import industries of all those countries were disrupted. As trade represented a significant percentage of GDP of those economies, protectionist trade policies ended up causing massive economic disequilibrium.

Unlike the 1930's, the huge standard of living difference between the developed world and the developing world is the most significant force driving trade today. In the 1930's, comparative advantage was the driving force of trade. Today, low wages in developing countries have created a competitive advantage for the developing world that is unmatched in history. Comparative advantage and competitive advantage can be quite different when used to determine the advantages of free trade.

When Adam Smith espoused the benefits of free trade, access to slave labor was not mentioned as a comparative advantage of any producing nation at that time. Comparative advantage was derived when one nation had the ability to produce a good or service more efficiently than another. Efficiency was usually due to the ease of access to a natural resource such as farm land, or mineral resources which in turn allowed the worker to learn the properties of the natural resource and work them for his benefit.

CHAPTER 4

When the natural resource of a nation was farmland, it made sense that the workers would be farmers who learned how to rotate crops and manage the soil in other ways. When the natural resource was a metal, it made sense for the workers to mine and create other products out of that metal. The farmers needed metals to be more productive and the metal workers needed food to eat. When each of these groups was allowed to pursue its most productive activity through use of trade, the world became a more productive place with everyone winning.

Adam Smith's productivity was determined by how much product could be produced with a unit of labor. Each unit of product and each unit of labor were the same standard measure in each competing country. While extolling the virtues of free trade today, many experts have exchanged the term of comparative advantage for competitive advantage. The standardized cost of a unit of labor has been replaced with a variable cost of a unit of labor. This change has bastardized Adam Smith's concept of the benefits of free trade.

Productivity now became determined by how much product could be produced by the cost of labor to produce the product. By changing the standard, the measurement of comparative advantage is lost. For example, if one country can produce 1 pound of copper by utilizing 1 hour of labor and another country can produce 1 pound of copper utilizing 2 hours of labor, which country has the comparative advantage? (Obviously, 1 hour to produce 1 pound is 50% comparatively better than 2 hours of labor to produce 1 pound). Does the same country have a comparative advantage if labor costs in the 2 hour country are 1/3 the labor costs of the 1 hour country? The cost of labor to produce 1 pound in the 2 hour country will be 66+% of the labor cost in the 1 hour country. If labor is the only determining factor in copper production, then the 2 hour country has a competitive advantage but not a comparative advantage. It will still be more efficient to produce copper in the 1 hour country. The fact that workers are willing to work for less in one country does not necessarily mean that the most efficient means of world production will be employed if competitive advantage drives production. If production is less efficient, then the intellectual argument for free trade based on competitive advantage loses its luster.

The differential in the price of labor today (and also other business costs such as regulation and property costs) between the developed and underdeveloped countries is so great that although developed countries may have a comparative advantage in many industries, in almost all industries they are at a competitive disadvantage. Free trade will result in more and more production going overseas until this competitive disadvantage disappears. As production goes overseas, so will jobs. When wages start to equalize this trend will end. Due to the massive disparity in wages, the equalization point will mean wages in the developed world will be substantially lower than they are today. The Western World's standard of living will fall dramatically!

The pundits of free trade claim this will not happen. Yet, when examining the effects of competitive advantage vs. comparative advantage in the case of free trade with Japan

from the early 1950's to the mid-1980s, we can see that serious problems developed. In the 1950s, trade with Japan
was inconsequential and their cheap goods were laughed
at by Americans as being such poor products. Their cheap
goods were produced by very cheap labor. Yet, these goods
were bought by Americans and produced a trade surplus
for Japan. This trade surplus was invested by Japanese businesses to create better export products to further capital-
ize on the Japanese competitive advantage of cheap labor.
The Japanese trade surplus grew enormously to over $100B
a year in the 1980s. Among the industries hardest hit were
the auto industry which would have failed without government intervention. And, the semi-conductor industry was
being pricing out of business along with many other manufacturing industries. Luckily, Japan's wage rate in 30 years
rose to somewhat comparable U.S. rates. The Japanese could
no longer rely on competitive advantage and comparative
advantage came into play. With this change the Japanese
economic threat died.

Japan's population was only about 1/3 of the U.S. population. Yet, their competitive advantage caused serious economic dislocations in the U.S. economy. Japan's competitive advantage started in the early 1950s and took about 15
years to become disruptive. The competitive advantages of
the developing countries today started first with the disin-
tegration of the Soviet Union in 1989. The peoples of the
Soviet bloc nations had been living in poverty for about 70
years under communism and its economic rationing system. The Soviet standard of living was less that 30% that of

the Western World. Its population's work force is about 25% greater than that of the U.S. The biggest problem posed by the breakup was the assimilation of East Germany by West Germany which resulted in a $1 trillion dollar bill for the West Germans.

The breakup of the Soviet Union initially resulted in the dominated countries spending 10 years to politically stabilize their countries and their economies. In the early 2000s, these countries became a place for U.S. companies to hire computer programmers for outsourcing of computer software work. This outsourcing helped put a lid on wages in the some of the highest paying jobs in the U.S. Where a U.S. programmer was making over $100K/year, the eastern European counterpart was paid at 1/10 that rate. This wage disparity has narrowed to about 30% but is still affecting U.S. workers. Luckily, the former soviet countries aimed at rebuilding their economies for domestic consumption and commodity exports. Since U.S. consumer industries were not under attack from these economies, the economic disruption caused by the wage differential hasn't been enormous.

In the mid 90's, China changed its communistic economic policies to become more profit motivated. The Chinese people had been economically dominated for centuries by their emperors, foreign powers, and then the communists. Slave labor was truly in place before the Chinese government changed their attitude toward capitalism. Over 1 billion people were released from their bonds with this change. The Chinese government realized that massive investment was needed in order to raise the Chinese standard of living and bring the country into the modern world.

Their economic plans targeted the consumer markets of the Western World since consumer goods represented the largest market of the Western World. Also, the technology to make most of these goods was low-tech and mostly required cheap labor. Because the price of Chinese labor was so low, the Chinese had a huge competitive advantage on the Western World. Attracting foreign capital that recognized the massive profit potential of cheap goods was an easy task.

At first, foreign investment was weary of political risk and moved slowly in spite of the spectacular possible returns. As the high returns on investment became realized, and the protocol for foreign investment became easy, foreign investment dollars flowed in faster and faster. In the past 15 years trillions of investment dollars have flowed to China.

U.S. production of consumer goods has plummeted as businesses have moved their production lines to China. Apple employs over 500,000 in China. And, Jeffery Immult, CEO of GE and president of President Obama's Council on Jobs and Competitiveness just closed a U.S. plant that resulted in 50,000 new Chinese jobs. Free trade with China has resulted in massive economic problems for the rest of the world. The economic disequilibrium caused by a labor force almost twice that of the developed world, initially released to compete at slave labor wages, has created the economic devastation plaguing the Western World today. In the last 10 years, more than 42,000 factories in the U.S. have shut down eliminating over 5 million jobs. Unfortunately, the loss of those 5 million jobs did not result in a creation of 5 million better paying jobs. Instead, the government's social safety net took on the brunt of the economic problems caused by this loss of jobs.

The recent massive increase in U.S. government debt can be directly attributed to the U.S. policy of free trade. As U.S. workers lose jobs to foreign competition, U.S. workers' incomes are reduced which reduces taxes on wages paid to the government. In addition, government safety nets kick in to reduce the hardship experienced by out-of-work individuals. This double action of reducing revenue and increasing expense has caused the U.S. debt burden to rise to historically high levels.

Over the past 11 years, the U.S. has run a $6 trillion trade deficit. Total U.S. Government debt has gone up about $7.5 trillion in the past 11 years. Not only does this argument concerning current free trade policy make intuitive sense, the correlation between the sizes of the trade deficit and government debt adds credence to the argument. Allowing goods to be imported because cheap labor overseas makes them cheaper than U.S. manufactured goods doesn't make economic sense. There are minimum wage laws in the U.S. Also, there are many government social safety programs designed to prevent U.S. residents from falling below a certain standard of living. A free trade program that thrives only because foreign workers work for wages well below the U.S. poverty standards has caused the viability of programs aimed to protect U.S. citizens from economic hardship to be in serious jeopardy!

CHAPTER 4

As long as there is a substantial difference in the U.S. standard of living and that of the rest of the world, the current free trade policy will bankrupt the U.S. as the cost of social safety programs keeps increasing with each old job shipped overseas while tax revenue also declines. Significantly reducing the trade deficit will help solve America's economic problems. The financial crisis has not been the only culprit of American's economic malaise. Free trade has also been a major contributor.

DISCUSSION POINT 5
Solutions to the Trade Deficit

A review of trade numbers reveals that the U.S. had a $510 billion dollar trade deficit in 2011. Imported oil accounted for $327B while trade with China resulted in a $295B deficit. Let's discuss what can be done in regard to the deficit caused by imported oil.

Recent breakthroughs in energy acquisition technology has resulted in a massive increase in available U.S. energy resources. The U.S. not only has the ability to become self-sufficient in energy but also has the ability to become a large exporter of energy. With the proper government incentives, the development of these resources would happen much more quickly. Unfortunately, current government policies have not encouraged development of these resources. Obama's lengthy delayed approval of the TransCanadian Keystone gas pipeline is the latest example of political vs. economic policy.

Obama delayed approval of the bill to attract the vote of environmentalists. As there hasn't been public outrage at this dismissal of a project that would create over 50,000 jobs, his political maneuver seems to have been the right one. So instead of the U.S. acting to create 50,000 jobs while reducing dependence on foreign oil, our government has decided environmental issues are more important. The U.S. environmental movement in the past 20 years has been responsible for the decline in U.S. production of oil. This decline has caused our trade deficit to balloon. When oil was at $20/barrel, maybe the U.S. could afford the luxury of environmental concerns.

However, economic times have changed and therefore priorities must be re-evaluated. If the standard of living in the world is expected to rise, then world pollution will rise (the standard of living is closely tied with energy consumption) as long as fuel technology doesn't become more efficient. A clean air standard in one country will only provide a competitive advantage for other countries who don't have the higher standard. This will lead only to wealth transfer without environmental benefit.

The environmental movement should consider this fact. And, U.S. citizens should be informed about the pros and cons of present environmental policy in regard to cleanness and its economic consequences. Current environmental issues are significantly hampering the development of new U.S. energy acquisition technology that could eliminate at least half the U.S. trade deficit while creating a massive amount of jobs. An important step in maintaining the U.S. standard of living is available. U.S. citizens must choose whether to accept a reduction in their standard of living or to take a chance on new technologies that might have a negative environmental impact.

Currently, foreign trade deficit dollars are going overseas and those citizens are using the money to decide whether a higher standard of living is more important than environmental issues. The biggest recipients of these dollars are the Chinese. In the past 10 years, they have been the worst polluters of the environment while they have drastically increased the use of carbon fuels to sustain the rise in their citizens' standard of living. And as pollution standards are almost non-existent in China, the environmental damage caused by increases in the standard of living there will be comparably much higher than in the U.S.

If U.S. environmental policy makes U.S. goods more costly and less competitive, those goods will be produced where the environment will be harmed to a greater degree. Government trade policy, environmentalists, and the consumer need to understand that cheap goods from the developing countries have unregulated hidden costs that are not allowed in the U.S. Holding only Americans liable for this cost will only cause jobs to go overseas, the American standard of living to go down, and not result in a cleaner world.

Without reducing the U.S. dependence on imported oil by initiating programs to accelerate the production of our oil and gas resources using new technology, the U.S. trade deficit will continue to weaken the economy. And, the owners of the dollars going overseas will be determining world environmental issues not the U.S. government or its people.

So although there is environmental risk in proceeding with a new technology, the current environmental policies of the governments receiving trade deficit dollars would indicate acceleration of new technology in the U.S. would be more environmentally friendly.

Let's discuss the second issue of America's trade problem and deficit with China. When the old communistic policies in China were changed in the mid-1990s and a more capitalistic system was introduced, their citizens wanted a better life. The Chinese wanted what Americans and their Western World colleagues had, a much higher standard of living. The average per capita income in China in the mid-1990s was about $500 (6000RMB x 08.25 – conversion rate of 8.25 renminbi to the dollar). The average U.S. per capita income was about $27,000 for the same period. Not only were Chinese wages a tiny faction (2%) of U.S. wages but also China didn't have child labor laws, safety nets for the poor, worker safety laws, environmental laws or many other costly government imposed restrictions on doing business. In addition, the cost of land and building production facilities was extremely low. With these advantages, China could easily compete with U.S. labor for jobs and capital. As long as American policy makers didn't find it unfair (to American workers) for American companies to hire slave labor outside the U.S., to provide the mechanism for cheap and free flowing financing to domestic companies building there, and to allow the export of goods produced by these companies back to America without trade restrictions, it was an easy decision for American companies to invest in China.

CHAPTER 4

The Chinese were more than happy to accept U.S. investment and the free trade policy as this was the perfect solution to improve the economic condition demanded by the Chinese people. This American free trade policy has cost the U.S. 5 million jobs and a huge trade deficit. China has gained better living conditions for their citizens and has also used their trade surplus to buy massive natural resource assets of other countries (including the U.S.). Letting the free trade policy continue will result in America losing its wealth and becoming another third world country.

The Chinese are assaulting the American way of life with every good that is sold that causes a job loss. Chinese goods are sold under the guise that cheap goods are beneficial to the average U.S. citizen because now they can purchase more goods. However, the cost of U.S. job losses is not added to the price of the cheap Chinese product. The toll on U.S. safety net programs is not added to the cost. And, the multiplier effect of each job loss on the rest of the U.S. economy is not accounted for. Additionally, the Chinese are using their U.S. trade surplus to buy claims on natural resources throughout the world. This buying has driven up commodity asset prices which has also hurt the average U.S. citizen. Gasoline prices have tripled in the past 10 years due to Chinese demand for oil. The U.S. is losing an economic war with China. And, even though the U.S. can end the war with a different trade policy, it has not chosen to do so.

Most products imported from China were previously produced in the U.S. What vital industrial product are we now importing from China that was unavailable under the old communistic system? The answer is 'None". The reason our trade deficit is so high with China is that the profit margin for arbitraging the low cost of Chinese labor against the relatively high cost of U.S. products manufactured by expensive U.S. labor is irresistibly high. Multi-national companies are making so much money that they want this activity to last as long as possible. If multi-national companies were making the majority of profits from building up the Chinese infrastructure or building plant and equipment related to selling product to the Chinese citizens, the trade deficit may not exist at all. Instead, the corporate profits are largely coming from selling products to Americans that are now produced in China that were previously produced in the U.S. Our country's economic problems are directly tied to this type of free trade.

And, the economic problems get compounded as more U.S. manufacturing goes overseas. The U.S. becomes less competitive for two reasons. One is that innovation comes from understanding how a product is manufactured. If products are manufactured abroad, there will be no domestic innovation in regard to that product. Secondly, many industries are linked together by their suppliers or supply chain. The supply chain of most products requires many suppliers of different products. As more industries go overseas, the number of domestic suppliers diminish and the remaining suppliers become less competitive. For example, if two different products are needed to produce another unique product and the two products need to be integrated in one place, then the country that can produce both products will have an advantage over the country only able to produce one of the products. One of the reasons for Apple moving its production of the IPhone to China was that the Chinese supply chain was better than the U.S. supply chain. As you can deduce, under the current free trade policy, the U.S. is on the road to ruin. Currently the largest 9 categories of net imports from China are:

1. Electrical machinery and equipment .. $78.5B
2. Power generation equipment $71.5B
3. Apparel $28.8B
4. Furniture $20.0B
5. Footwear $15.9B
6. Iron & Steel $8.4B
7. Leather $7.5B
8. Plastics $4.8B
9. Optical & Medical equipment $1.8B

The first 2 categories of net imports show clearly that China is fabricating essential elements of products that are finished in the U.S.

Because China has become so integrated in the production of important U.S. products, it would be impossible to immediately bring that production back to the U.S. However, a 5 year plan with incentives to do so would likely be workable. Bringing back key industries and key suppliers is essential to U.S. manufacturing survival. A 5 year plan to bring the Chinese trade deficit down to low double digits or single digits should be part of an American goal.

Also, immediately, the U.S. could demand payment for pirated intellectual property in the area of software and hardware infringement. And, industries 3-9 could be targeted for trade tariffs along with domestic incentives to rebuild those industries. To help counter the blow to China, the U.S. could agree to help create a credit card system for the Chinese consumer to stimulate Chinese consumer demand to replace the decline in its export business. Should the Chinese banks require access to additional capital to finance this lending, the U.S. could ease lending regulations to Chinese financial institutions. So instead of having to borrow from the Chinese to facilitate a trade deficit, they could borrow from us to facilitate their domestic consumption. In fact, our banks could lend to Chinese consumers who purchased U.S. goods. Unfortunately, in the past decade, it was the U.S. banks that facilitated the purchase of Chinese products to the U.S. consumer via credit card debt. Had the Chinese banks given the U.S. consumer credit, the U.S. banks wouldn't have lost their shirt in the credit crisis. The Chinese banks would have.

In order to move forward in resolving the economic disequilibrium now plaguing the U.S. and the Western World, the current free trade policy has to be ended. In addition, the discovery of the new technology that taps into natural energy resources must be utilized immediately. There is a currently a glut of natural gas that has depressed its price to an absurd level. Currently, natural gas is trading about $4 per thousand cubic feet. A barrel of oil is selling at around $100/barrel. The energy equivalent of 5.8 thousand cubic feet of natural gas is one barrel of oil. So natural gas is priced at the equivalent of less than $23/barrel vs. one barrel of oil at around $100/barrel even though it is a much cleaner fuel.

In Japan and Western Europe, natural gas is trading at over $14 per thousand cubic feet. The U.S. price is low because the domestic and international distribution network for this natural gas is inadequate. In order to speed up the process of bring this gas to market, congress needs to pass the Natural Gas Act (H.R. 1834 and S.1408) along with many other incentives. A leader in the energy field, Boone Pickens has produced a plan that could be a model for these incentives. The benefits of energy independence would not only be a reduction in the deficit but also be instrumental in significant job growth in the U.S.

The main reason that the current free trade policy exists is two-fold. Many politicians have been convinced that the Adam Smith theory and argument for free trade is as valid today as it was 250 years ago. Secondly, multi-national corporations are making enormous profits by producing cheap goods overseas and are politically active to ensure that the free trade policy remains in place. It is unfortunate that politicians and the managers of these corporations are so short sighted not to see that their actions will lead to the collapse of the American (and European) consumer markets as consumer demand, reliant on good wages, dries up. The economic disequilibrium caused by arbitraging cheap labor has already resulted in trillion dollar bailouts of both the U.S. and European economies by government entities. If allowed to persist, an economic depression will occur. Then, the short-term corporate profits currently driving stock prices (and manager compensation) will turn massively negative and these same corporations will face bankruptcy.

The government policy allowing free trade is as bad as the recent government policy of maximizing American home ownership. Free trade is being subsidized by the taxpayer in the form of massively increased governmental social safety net expenses paid to laid-off workers whose jobs have gone overseas. The home ownership policy was subsidized by the government instigating lower federal (Fannie Mae and Freddie Mac) home loan standards. In each case, the government and all those in favor of these policies chose to focus on the short-term benefits while ignoring the historical evidence indicating that the policies being implemented would result in catastrophic failure. The public, both political parties, and the stewards of business were instrumental in pushing for a maximum ratio of U.S. citizen home ownership. The short term rewards for those interested parties were substantial as home prices rose with increased demand, stock prices went up, and hundreds of millions of dollars went to the corporate stewards and their political allies.

Now the public is the one paying the price. However, the responsibility for that stupid loan policy has been dumped on the financial entities themselves (by politicians and the press) not the politicians or the C-level executives and their Boards who were responsible for implementation of the bad policy. Also, the public is being duped into believing that most financial institutions are owned by 'fat cats' who need to be punished. The truth is that the public through their pension fund investments are the real owners of these companies. And, these shareholders and bondholders lost their shirts while those actually responsible took home loads of cash. The irony of the political press is that the indignation against the irresponsible policies of financial institutions is being cast on the owners not the decision makers of these companies. The major losers (owners) are being castigated for being so irresponsible while the winners (management) are walking away scot-free.

Currently, the stewards of multi-national corporations and their political allies are following the strategy of substituting foreign labor for domestic labor in the production of goods to be sold domestically. By severely compromising the domestic labor market, these companies are undercutting the source of demand (due to low wages) for their domestic product. This short-term corporate strategy has resulted in rising current profits. And, stock prices are soaring because of these larger profits. Decision making executives who have large incentives tied to stock performance due to options granted in their contracts have embraced a short-sighted policy even at the risk of major long-term consequences. This is a repeat of their actions in the financial crisis. Just as executives' (and politicians') personal incentives drove them to approve ridiculous lending policies in the mid-2000's, the incentives from free trade are causing them to back this bad policy also. The public again will be footing the bill for the likely future disaster coming due to free trade.

In regard to the government's U.S. energy policy, it's easy to see how politicians are playing the environmental movement to stifle development of U.S. energy resources. By creating new rules and regulations, the government becomes even more powerful as it gains control of the tremendously large new resource that can change the U.S. economic status quo. New rules and regulations will create new government agencies to oversee the new technology of the oil industry. New taxes and fees will be implemented. And, the size of government, along with its corresponding power, will grow. This is the politician's fantasy.

The U.S. has the resources, the technology, and the manpower to maintain the current standard of living of its citizens. The country is rich in resources and human talent. The U.S. has an abundant amount of resources to export to exchange for whatever few resources that need to be imported. If the U.S. government changed its current free trade policy that creates huge trade deficits to a fair trade policy that would allow only small trade deficits, the return of many industries and jobs shipped and outsourced overseas would occur. And if the new energy technology was encouraged by government action instead of impeded, U.S. economic growth would soar. Positive government policies in regard to these two elements of the economy would return America to full employment. America would resume its rightful place as the leading economic power and freedom leader of the world.

The solution to returning America to greatness needs to be implemented. Why isn't America moving in that direction? How is it that the head of the Federal Reserve and majority of its members don't get it? And, how is it that the President and Congress don't get it? And, why isn't foreign competition being discussed especially after Donald Trump received huge public approval ratings for his stance to face down the Chinese in the 2012 Presidential primaries? The author guesses that all the same elite who ignored common sense by allowing financial institutions to implement ridiculously low borrowing standards is the same group of people and institutions who are equally ignorant of understanding the current woes of the U.S. economy. Or, again, does common sense get in the way of special interest groups who want to game the American public again for larger profits?

Addendum 1 - Additional Discussion About Free Trade

Since there will be many attacks on the ideas presented in this book, especially concerning free trade, a simple hypothetical circumstance might be helpful to persuade the critics and help the average reader understand the problem with free trade today.

Assume only two countries exist in the world and each had exactly the same natural resources and landmass. Also, assume that the populations of each country had an equal distribution of educated people. In regard to each countries' standard of living, which country would be more likely to have a higher standard of living, the country having 300 million people or the country having 1.3 billion people, assuming there was an impassable natural barrier between countries? It's quite obvious that the country with the higher ratio of resources to population would have the higher standard of living (assumption – natural resources are not unlimited).

THE LAST YEARS OF FREEDOM

Historically, many countries enjoyed higher standards of living than other countries. War and conquest was a method used to increase a country's standard of living and decrease the differential. In this hypothetical case, historically without natural barriers, the country with the larger population would conquer the smaller populated country and the wealth of 1.6 billion people would be distributed resulting in a drastic decline in the wellbeing of the 300 million people. Today, economic war is being waged with free trade that will result in the same outcome. The redistribution of goods of the wealthy 300 million will result in the destruction of America and the American Dream. As free trade benefits a small minority, the stratification of wealth and power will increase. And, as in every country where this has occurred, the wealthy and politically powerful will put a strangle hold on the rest of society. This includes communistic countries where power is stratified in the communist party's political system. And, its leaders have lead magnificent lifestyle by having access to any and all of their country's resources.

CHAPTER 5

Special Interests, Political Parties and Their Propaganda

The leaders of both our political parties are excellent manipulators using the current crisis as a way to increase power for themselves and their parties. Their propaganda is powerful. These parties now control a government that directs expenditures of 38% of the GDP. Unfortunately for our free society, they want to control more!! There are no ethical boundaries for these parties. They will fabricate any message or story to make fantasy seem like reality. Just as special effects have made the impossible real in the movies, the new social media has made impossible political claims seem truthful. Mass media has played a huge role in influencing the voter with political propaganda ads and stories. The power grab is evident from both parties.

Left wing propaganda plays on the knowledge that people don't like being the less privileged in society. Their leaders know that a disparity in economic circumstances causes strife between groups in society. Jealousy is a very powerful human characteristic. The fact that some individuals are wealthier than others is a cause for jealousy. The jealousy trait is used to manipulate the less privileged to vote for the left's party candidate and political agenda.

SPECIAL INTERESTS -
POLITICAL PARTIES AND THEIR PROPAGANDA

Today's left wing leaders are using the jealousy factor to create a class warfare program to promote their election to power. Today, as in the past, the cry from the left is that the disparity between the rich and the poor is unjust and unfair. The left leadership states that it represents the working class as well as the unfairly downtrodden. They assert the claim that the average worker is responsible for most of the goods and services produced in the economy. Being responsible for this production entitles the worker to most of the goods produced according to liberal theory.

Although the argument seems to have merits of logic and therefore has gained general acceptance among the population, a historical review of productivity gains due to innovation reveals that this argument is lacking in credibility. The truth is that a miniscule fraction of the population is responsible for the standard of living that exists in western civilization today. Societies that rewarded those innovators and their inventions have reaped the benefit of every type of economic and societal advancement.

The reason America has reached the status of the most prolific nation on earth is due to its policy of promoting risk taking by individuals who hope to obtain significant wealth. Seeking rich rewards, entrepreneurs and inventors created new products and more efficient ways of building older products. These achievements resulted in productivity gains that propelled America to be the largest economy on earth. Although most Americans work hard, which is a product of the Puritan ethic, the added productivity from a hard-working man vs. a lazy man is within the single digit multiple of one. Inventions and methods of using the wheel, the plow, iron, steel, the windmill, electricity, motorized vehicles, the computer, etc. increased the productivity of man from many times to thousands of times. Entrepreneurs and inventors were solely responsible for this, not the average working man!

Successful inventors and innovators are rare among the population. Political and economic systems that heavily rewarded these individuals were the societies responsible for man's escape from the jungle and for the living standard we enjoy today. All workers should bow down in gratefulness to those responsible for their good life! Instead, the left attempts to distort the truth by telling the average worker he is responsible for all the goods produced by the economy. This propaganda is aimed at convincing the average worker that he has equal worth in relation to the successful inventor, innovator, and entrepreneur.

In the past, most Americans believed that a superior work ethic or superior brain power that benefited all Americans needed to be rewarded. And the reward endowed on those who exhibited their superiority (which caused wages and the standard of living to increase for all Americans) was considered fair. Americans believed that these individuals were entitled to at least a significant share of the bigger pie that they created. And, the working man was happy that the amount of pie he got kept growing.

In the last few years, the amount of pie that the average working man has received has diminished. The left has recognized this and created a propaganda campaign that plays on the working man's emotional state and man's instinct to be jealous. It is easy to promote the blame game in spite of contrary empirical evidence when emotions are running high. The left has run a superior campaign of misleading propaganda to convince the American worker that somehow the rich cheated or were given unfair advantages to achieve their wealth. By creating an image that the American working man has equally contributed to the wealth of the nation, the left's propaganda lends credence to its argument that wealth needs to be shared for fairness sake. The left totally ignores discussing the economic consequences that will befall the country when the incentives for superior intellect and working abilities are diminished.

Right wing propaganda has focused on how capitalism and freedom have created an unparalleled political and economically successful nation. Their propaganda talks about the successful entrepreneur and the need to provide incentives for his continued success. This narrative was mostly true until professional business managers began to run big business and fractured ownership led to a loss of corporate control by the real business owners. Big business today is run by a Board of Directors and their hired guns, the executive team. The owners are pension funds and other retirement entities owned by the American public. The right wing party strongly supports this type of big business even though it is no longer an entrepreneurial enterprise.

The public which owns the majority interest in corporate America is interested in the long-term profitability of their companies. The corporate management in America may not necessarily share the same goal. A significant portion of this management's compensation is derived from stock options. Therefore, risk taking is promoted without the counter balance of loss. These executives don't have their own capital at risk. The current financial crisis can be attributed to the fiduciary irresponsibility of the financial sector. Banks made huge loans without collateral. Investment houses securitized these loans and sold them to institutional investors. The banks and investment houses made huge fees doing this and the institutional investors earned a higher than average rate of return on their investments. All these higher returns drove stock prices of corporate American companies higher. And, the management teams of these institutions made millions by exercising low priced options and selling the higher priced exchange traded stocks.

Although the shareholders of banks and investment houses, and the investors in institutional money management companies lost almost everything, the management teams that had followed imprudent, irresponsible business policies became extremely wealthy by having a participating interest when things were good but not being liable for a percentage of the losses when the shit hit the fan.

The Republican propaganda promoting the inventor and entrepreneur as the main beneficiaries of their political agenda is incorrect as their support of big business run for the benefit of elitist management has little in common with true entrepreneurial capitalism.

The propaganda of both the Republicans and the Democrats blames the other side for the economic failure of the last few years. And, each party continues to add to the enormous power shared by controlling the political system in an ever larger government. The two party system is a duopoly that controls the American public. The financiers of this system are the public unions for the Democrats, and big business for the Republicans. The propaganda that these parties espouse is used to hide the real issues while still appearing to be having an agenda to benefit the public. Just as the propaganda of both parties is misleading so are their stated agendas. The problems facing America today have not been caused by the rich entrepreneur or inventor or the discrepancy in wealth between the rich and the poor. And, although government entitlement programs have gotten out of hand, they are only a part of the reason for America's economic malaise.

Big business's arbitrage of selling cheap foreign products (made with the equivalent of slave labor in former communist countries) to American consumers while undercutting American-made products has been the major cause of the current economic turmoil. Millions of jobs have been lost to foreign competition causing massive extensions of support programs and federal deficits. As the government, supported by the political parties, has extended aid and entitlements to the workers of the suffering economy, this has provided the financial backing for the consumer necessary to prolong the arbitrage. The arbitrage in the short run continues to enrich corporate America and its corporate elite. It also enriches the politicians and the two political parties by increasing their power to endow government funds and to control regulations that benefit special interest groups as the size of the government increases. Thus both the Republican and the Democratic parties have a vested interest in continuing the policy of Free Trade. And, relief for the unemployed will continue to bolster government power. The 'Financial Crisis' is playing the scapegoat role for the bad economy as politicians use it to gain further influence over America's free society.

DISCUSSION POINT 1
80 Years of Political Power Grab - Evidence of the Real Agenda of the Republican and Democratic Parties

The Democratic and Republican political parties have been responsible for the huge growth in government, mega corporations, and massive unions. Since Franklin D. Roosevelt became President in 1932, unprecedented power in these power structures has continually grown. Government spending has grown as a percentage of the GDP from 12% in 1928 to 30% in the early 1950s and to around 40% today. 40% of this country's resources have been diverted away from production to the non-productive administration of government. Government unions and big business have been the main beneficiary of this unstoppable trend.

On the business side, cities and towns with mom and pop stores and local banks have been replaced with national banks and national chain shopping stores and centers. Good paying jobs at stores delivering domestic product have been replaced with low paying jobs that deliver foreign product. The wage differential of a senior corporate executive and that of an average worker has soared from 20/1 to over 200/1.

SPECIAL INTERESTS -
POLITICAL PARTIES AND THEIR PROPAGANDA

Owner run companies that understood the contribution of its executives were replaced by shareholder corporations run by The Board of Directors. And, these Directors, usually composed of elite executives, created industry standards as a method to justify the stair stepping of C- level compensation to the current rarified levels

In regard to the unions, union power shifted from the private sector to the government sector to include the Teacher's, Fireman's, Police Unions, and other public worker unions. As government employees in the 1950s, teachers, firemen, policemen, and other public workers had job security but were paid a salary somewhat lower than offered by the private sector. Union power in recent years has been used to advocate for higher salaries and benefits, through political initiatives, that became many times higher than paid to private industry workers. These compensation plans today are consuming such a high portion of local and state budgets that many states and municipalities could file for bankruptcy in the not too distant future in the event of any adverse economic event (States owe $4.19T including pension under-funded liabilities which represents 123% of their yearly revenues. On the municipality level, according to Morningstar 30% of the top 25 major cities in the U.S. fall below their fiscally sound threshold).

Public worker union power and executive corporate power has grown hand-in-hand with government's growth. These three power structures have worked together to push government spending to unsustainable levels. The economic policies and regulatory policies that these entities have put in place are bankrupting the country and creating the huge disparity of wealth between the rich and poor. Wealth is flowing to the administrators of these entities.

The union bosses are very wealthy because of the power and influence they control. The big business corporate managements at the C level to the Board level are massively wealthy. And, the government politicians have also taken their share of wealth. If the policies promoted by these individuals controlling the country resulted in good and reliable growth in our country's wealth production, these individuals would have earned their compensation. Unfortunately, the policies that have been instituted at their direction have led us down the road to poverty. The average citizen has given up many Constitutional rights and has become reliant on the Big Three Power structures to advocate for an increase in his standard of living. Self-reliance has almost disappeared and with it, America's standard of living is in trouble.

DISCUSSION POINT 2 -
Continuing Down the (Un)Progessive Road of Government

The successful progression of the US economy in the past has been the effort of creative individuals not big government, big business or big labor. In spite of the obstacles put in place by these large entities, small innovative businesses have created almost all the growth (70% of all new private jobs created in the last 30 years) in the U.S. Yet, current policies do not incentivize small business. Instead there is more government oversight into business practices and personal life choices resulting in a massive increase in power in these three entities and a reduction in civil liberties and employment opportunities of the average American.

President Obama was elected in 2008 on the promise that he would change the government way of doing business. The government would be more responsive to the people by reducing lobbying, reducing earmarks, and answering the call of the people. Unfortunately, this did not happen. Instead, the President decided his ideas were more important than those of the people. His agenda has been to increase the size of the federal government with massive new spending programs such as health care, and to increase federal government oversight into immigration, gay marriage, abortion, green energy, and finance. In spite of massive protests about his policies, none of his agenda was changed or included compromises. President Obama's policies have been contrary to his promises and to the interests of the American people.

In regard to his heath care program, Obamacare was legislated in spite of massive protests. 20,000 pages of legislation was passed without overview by the legislators (virtually no member in Congress read the bill and Nancy Pelosi, the Speaker of the House at the time said "We have to pass this bill to see what's in it."). In order to get the bill passed, Obama had to make many back door side deals with legislators. The public and their representatives didn't want this legislation. In spite of the president's and the Democratic Party's promises to the contrary, Obamacare is much more expensive to the nation and is putting a large burden on small business. Insurance companies have cancelled over 4 million affordable policies because they didn't meet Obamacare standards. Because insurance companies are compelled to offer insurance unnecessary to the majority of individuals, tailored more affordable plans have been required to be scrapped. As a result, the cost of insurance to the individual and small companies has risen by over 25%. This is killing small business.

In regard to big business, the Dodd-Frank Bill has reduced the competitiveness of small banks by increasing the cost of business. The behemoth banks have gotten bigger than before the financial crisis. Instead of being punished for irresponsible lending behavior, the government stepped in, bailed them out and introduced oversight laws that gave them a bigger competitive advantage. Instead of punishing the executives that directed the imprudent banking policies, the executives at failed banks were given golden parachutes when their banks were merged while the more subsidized larger merger banks' executives got more stock options. This legislation is a slap in the face of those initially injured (shareholders, bondholders, and borrowers) by the irresponsible actions of elite executives. The legislation incorporated no punitive action against the irresponsible while still favoring the big banks over the small banks.

On another front, the government's promoted low interest rate policy enacted to stimulate the economy has been massively beneficial to the behemoth U.S. international companies not small businesses. U.S. banks have not lent to the small U.S. business but have opened their bank vaults to lend to the gigantic corporations. Unfortunately, rates of return overseas have been much higher than in the U.S. So, the loans to U.S. multi-national corporations have flowed overseas to the higher returns. And, middle-class Americans with trillions in money market funds have been left holding the bag with having to invest with savings rates at an unbelievable low of .25%. And, the U.S. jobs that should have been created by low interest rates moved to the Far East. An additional negative is that those new Far East jobs are adding to the competitiveness of the Eastern world against small U.S. businesses.

On the union front, more government means more government workers. And, more workers provide more monetary and political power to the unions and their bosses. More government workers mean higher taxes and more regulation. It also means cronies of big labor executives will get some contracts that might otherwise have gone to unaffiliated small businesses due to union influence.

The growth of government, big business, and big labor has resulted in massive resources being entrusted to a few individuals. The history of mankind has shown that concentrated power never is beneficial to the masses. The current governmental policies, large business practices, and large union demands, are not in the interests of the American public. Their implementation has been detrimental to small businesses. These policies have been advocated mainly for the benefit of the head administrators of the three entities discussed.

CHAPTER 5

The concentration of power has become too large. Billions of dollars are now required to win a presidential election and hundreds of millions are required for governorship and congressional elections. All of this money is used to produce propaganda to sway the public vote. This money can only be raised through the two political parties who have access to the big money contributors who have special interests. These special interest groups are heavily staked into the current system. America has arrived at a very unfortunate moment in its history. Its main political parties have succeeded in creating a powerful political and economic structure that is stifling not only individual freedom but economic prosperity as well. The only road back to freedom and a vibrant economy will by changing the power structure willfully created by the Republican and Democratic parties for the last 80 years. That will take time. A more immediate threat to Americans needs to be addressed at once, the continuing advancement of socialism in America.

The Threat of American Socialism
Independence from Government is Freedom, Socialistic Reliance is Servitude

The political power grab of the last 80 years by both the Democratic and Republican Parties is responsible for a bloated, anti-entrepreneurial government. As bad as the state of government prior to 2008 had become, the election of the Democrats to power in 2008 made the situation much worse. A full-fledged campaign to gain total governmental control is now underway with President Obama leading the charge. The Democrats want full control of all bodies of government to promote their socialistic agenda without interference. They don't want a bi-partisan government which would dilute their power. And, solving America's current economic problems is a very low priority.

The Democrats want to change America from a somewhat free capitalist country to a country run by a socialist (if not communist) regime. And, the Democratic Party is showing it doesn't care what tactics are pursued for this end. 2013 has brought to light government implemented cover-up scandals such as Bengazi (an attempt to hide evidence that governmental foreign policy isn't succeeding), the IRS targeting of some members of the Tea Party from 2010 onward (to discourage anti-Democratic opposition), and journalists investigations (to discourage journalistic criticism of Democratic policies). These are a few instances of the Democrats using their power abusively and unlawfully. Other instances include Eric Holder's handling of Fast and Furious, associations with radical political groups and people, and radical interpretations of Constitutional Law and Congressional Ruling Body Law.

So, although both political parties have gained tremendous power in the last 8 decades by working together to reformulate the American Dream, the struggle for ultimate governmental control is now taking place. The Democrats want to gain total control of our monolith government to make America a totally socialistic country whereas the Republicans think a ration of capitalism is still a good thing. Each party has become much too powerful and therefore is a menace to the American Dream. And, as each Party's primary concern is to increase their power base, their solutions to solve American economic woes are bastardized by this concern. The Democratic agenda however would have dire consequences.

The preface of this book was a narrative of the likely outcome if the Democratic Party's current power grab attempt succeeds. That outcome would lead America to communism and therefore failure. The election of President Obama seems to foreshadow this happening. How could this come to pass in what was the most capitalistic country in the world? And will the American economy sink under the weight of absolute government where politicians promote policies to increase their own power instead of the wellbeing of the nation? A process started in the 1960's reveals the beginnings of this danger and its impact on America.

After the Vietnam War, the U.S. educational system was overrun with anti-war (left wing) socialistic minded teachers. And, since the liberal arts graduates of that system became the majority of reporters and writers for today's major media outlets (national TV networks and national newspapers), socialistic propaganda has spewed from them poisoning the minds of many average Americans (especially the young).With liberal ownership of much of the media, there has been no check on the assumptions and facts underlying the content of this liberal journalism. Through these commentators, unchecked left wing idealistic ideas have been espoused as the 'correct way of thinking' in spite of their historical failure in actual practice. The teaching and media community have had a tremendous impact on voters, many of which have accepted their writings as gospel (36% of Americans believe in the concept of socialism). And, more and more local, state, and federal laws have been passed to make government the most important entity in American society. Fifty years of media propaganda has resulted in a very strong backing for socialistic governmental policies by the American public.

As American government adopts more and more socialistic policies, the dangers of that route to society and the economy aren't mentioned by the media or educators. Instead, these supposed champions (journalists and teachers) of exposing the truths and lies in society are those instead who continue to promote the lie of socialism which relies on a concept of fairness and sharing that doesn't exist in nature or the nature of man.

The following discussions will expose the underlying assumptions of socialism as false, thereby exposing its actual practice as detrimental to society in general and America in particular.

DISCUSSION POINT 1
Socialistic Fairness and Sharing Concepts

The most basic premise underlying the philosophy of socialism is that any large inequality of ownership or unequal consumption of goods by individuals in society is wrong and unfair. Socialists believe this unfairness is the major reason for the strife and unhappiness in society. In socialism, fair is mainly defined as having distribution of somewhat equal shares of production and wealth regardless of contribution. This type of fairness doesn't exist in nature. The weak and uncommon members of the animal world are either killed by or cast out of the animal group. The strongest and smartest get the 'lions' share of food and their choice of a mate or mates. There is no equality of sharing! And, those who can't produce die. And, in man, the same self-interested behavior and lack of caring for the underachiever has been dominant in all societies.

Mankind has produced a history of prejudice, slavery, conquest, and power and wealth for the elite (smartest and strongest members of society). The common man throughout history has taken his subordinate place below his leaders accepting the behavior of allegiance and subordination required of him. He expected to get what his rank deserved, less than those above him but more than those below. Fairness was getting what your rank commanded. In most of these societies, rank was mostly determined at birth by family status. In a very few societies, individual merit was highly valued in determining an individual's rank in society. Even in those few societies (Greeks, American Indian, etc.) which allowed individual merit to determine rank, there was never a belief that the members of all ranks of those societies should share either power or wealth equally.

The socialistic concept that wealth should be shared equally runs counter to the natural world's behavior. The implementation of such a concept must therefore be doomed to failure. Also, fairness as defined by the socialist doesn't exist in nature or human behavior. This artificial socialistic solution for creating happiness in mankind if conscripted by law therefore would also have to fail.

The question of why a society of equal sharing (or almost equally) sharing has never existed in large societies until 1917 should be asked of the liberal educators, liberal media, and liberal politicians. If this type of society worked best for its participants, why in the 10,000 years of civilization did it rarely exist? And, why after being tried in Russia, China, Eastern Europe, and Cuba for close to 80 years, was it such a failure?

Socialists have long argued that a system that strives for equality in wealth and power is the 'fairest of political systems'. Conjecture and idealistic thinking are not solutions in the real world. Putting bread on the table is. And, apparently for 10,000 years people thought the system of rank was a better system of putting food on the table than socialism. In the last 80 years, after the socialistic idealistic system was put in place, our ancestry was proved correct! Communism in Russia, the most radical form of socialism failed in 1989. Communism in China failed a few years later. These two massive, extensive, and lengthy programs to test the socialistic theory of wealth sharing produced massive decay not a vibrant society.

However, this evidence has been ignored as the propaganda machine of the media, educators, and left-wing politicians continues unabated. There has been no acknowledgement of the error in their thinking. Instead, the success of the capitalistic entrepreneur in creating enormous increases in productivity has simply been seen as causing a widening gap between the rich and the poor! The fact that the standard of living of the poor has dramatically increased hasn't been seen as important as the widening of the wealth gap. History has shown capitalism to be superior to socialism in bettering the human condition. The lies promoted by socialistic thinkers that government is good for society has and continues to further the implementation of an inferior system that history shows will fail.

DISCUSSION POINT 2
Socialism vs. Evolution

God created an infinite diversity of characteristics in man and an equal diversity in the abilities to harness those characteristics. In society, the honing of those characteristics created the civilized world we live in. Characteristics that fulfilled the demands of society were selected while those that didn't were discarded. The selection process resulted in those individuals with the desired skills being rewarded while those that didn't meet the standard were cast aside.

Unfortunately, God didn't create only individuals with the desired skill set! Let's label the group with the desired skill set achievers and the group without it the non-achievers. Achievers produce what society wants while non-achievers don't. Also, as part of God's basket of characteristics, self-interest and self-gratification were also included.

In order for society to obtain the most out of the achievers, it must provide the most gratifying rewards for the self-interested achiever. Money, wealth, and power (sex also) have been the historic reward system for man. And, as man is the most successful of all the animal species, this reward system's merits can't be contested as a poor system. The socialistic goal of income and wealth equality is completely lacking in similar rewards. The nebulous reward of a 'fair' society for those inspired by socialism is totally contrary to the reward system based on self-interest which has provided so much progress for mankind.

The joy of sharing doesn't cut it as a replacement for the self-interested reward system that society evolved for man. All highly socialistic societies are underachievers in fulfilling their citizens' needs because they have failed to produce a better reward system which doesn't include power, money and wealth. The failure to provide the right incentives for the achievers in Russia, China, Cuba, and other communist countries resulted in poverty for its citizens. Also, aristocracies or other government forms that only provided incentives for the elite greatly lagged in the economic development of their economies. The economies in Latin American and South Asian countries are prime examples as their standards of living are extremely lower than those of the Western World.

Note also that not only does the better reward system produce more goods for its citizens, but in doing so also creates a more compassionate atmosphere for the non-achiever. Successful societies produce a surplus of goods. The greater the surplus, the less reason there is to hoard those goods. Rich societies are therefore more tolerant. Also, the well-to-do citizens of these societies are willing to provide a higher standard of living for the non-achievers than in poor societies. Maslow's hierarchy of human needs provides the reason for this as wealthy individuals seek to fulfill spiritual needs and therefore view the poor in a better light. By replacing a successful reward system with the introduction of a failed reward system, those who advocate for extreme wealth sharing are dooming the non-achiever to the worst possible outcome, a lower standard of living and a less compassionate society.

In early times when societies were poor, the most unproductive became beggars and if they were lacking in begging skills, they died. Today in the developed countries, it is thought that nobody is worthless enough to let die. And, it is also thought that compassion helps a society become more cohesive. Wealthy societies with excess production have chosen to support the non-achievers with this view as the rewards from the karma of giving outweighs the diminished importance of having excess surplus. However, as the surplus owned by the achievers diminishes, they are much less inclined to give it away. As the measure of society's wealth decreases, the value of karma from giving also decreases which results in less giving.

If a society controlled by achievers changes to one controlled by non-achievers, production will decline as non-achievers will attempt to use their power to increase the percentage of their rewards from production. As achievers anticipate the rewards from their labor (and investment) will decline, this disincentive will cause the achiever to readjust his personal priorities away from production. All attempts to make achievers conform to giveaways to the government through taxes or to workers through regulations concerning the treatment of their workers (minimum wage laws, health-care benefits, etc.) will cause society's production to decline as achievers chose gratifying non-productive efforts to replace those of production. This is not a hard concept to understand as every aspect of society from family to the work environment uses incentive to motivate the individual. And, as incentives decrease, behavior attributed from those incentives is less influenced and vice-versa.

It's amazing that liberal educators and liberal media ignore or minimize the concept of incentive as a driving force for economic production, especially when their own personal lives revolve so much around this concept!!! In addition, socialists never acknowledge the huge differential in the production capabilities of the productive members of society vs. the non-productive members of society. This differential is due to God's gift to man in the form of diversity. Turning a blind eye to the truth, educators and the media still proclaim the virtues of socialism. This irresponsible behavior has resulted in voters believing in a failed unnatural system. America is on the brink of completing the process of implementing socialism as its political system thanks to some very incompetent intellectuals who hold sway over the public!

The War of Independence must be fought again. The aristocratic monarchy isn't the enemy this time, but the political juggernaut of socialism is. And, the Democratic Party is at its head! True Americans need to join the battle to convince the public that the bag of goodies being offered by the liberals is the same bag offered by con-artists. There is nothing but rocks inside.

DISCUSSION POINT 3
Darwinian Theory At Odds With Socialism

Most liberals believe the implementation of liberal ideas can make the world a better place. A significant concept associated with liberal ideas is that many citizens of the world are treated unfairly. And, laws need to be instituted to make the world a fairer place. In the liberals mind, although most discussion concerns economic welfare, the closer everyone is to having the same worldly goods, and the same physical and mental attributes, the closer mankind would be to nirvana. When everyone is equal, how can unfairness exist?

A case might be made for clones but that argument ignores the Darwinian theory of survival of the fittest. In Darwinian theory diversity in a species is essential for the survival of that species. So, if ultimate fairness is the prime objective of liberal policy, then if achieved the results may lead to extinction. Luckily, God created man with many different physical and mental attributes. Thus, allowing him to adapt to his environment and survive.

Unfortunately, man's diversification necessarily created the unfairness liberals are trying to rectify. History is the record of man taking for himself or his companions as much as possible with total disregard to fairness toward other fellow men. Unfair advantage determined the winners and losers. As man is the dominant and most successful animal species in the world, does it make sense to promote a policy to change man's use of unfair advantage? The 'survival of the fittest theory' suggests that inferior members of a species die leaving only the strongest to live and breed. Is this unfair? If so, shouldn't Mother Nature or God who created the inferior be blamed?

The conflict among men trying to use their unfair advantage has been the impetus that has driven societal and economic development. Almost everyone in the developed world lives better than the aristocracy of the 19th century. If the present concept of liberal fairness was prevalent in historic times, our species may not exist today and the western world's standard of living certainly wouldn't!

CHAPTER 6

DISCUSSION POINT 4
Community Sharing Trumps Self-Interest?

An underlying assumption of socialism is that the sharing of production (especially unequal sharing) is an acceptable practice among most members of society. Without majority acceptance of this socialistic tenant, many detrimental problems with production will occur as individuals attempt to evade sharing rules.

The actual behavior of individuals in society indicate that minimal sharing might be acceptable. However, since most individuals tally a fairness count in every relationship they maintain, the tolerance for unequal sharing is very low. An example of this tally is the calculation of the sum of money spent by each party of a relationship in joint outings (dinners, movies, etc. - birthday or Christmas gifts, etc. are also a subject of calculation) and the corresponding services received to determine if each party paid the appropriate share. The fairness tally for each relationship is a running total that takes into account the generous occasions in which one party pays the bill but expects reciprocal treatment sometime in the future. A vast majority of relationships fail when reciprocity doesn't occur and therefore the 'injured' party feels unfairly treated. Even in America's rich society, a couple of hundred dollars is often enough to destroy friendships! And, what brother or sister happily lends (gives) money to their lazy free-loading siblings?! The saying 'never lend money to family and friends' didn't just come to pass for no reason!

THE THREAT OF AMERICAN SOCIALISM

In all societies the counting behavior is equally prevalent at all levels. Neither the achievers nor the non-achievers want to contribute (share) more than they receive from others. They may be persuaded to share if confronted by a hostile group (pressure from family members, community or political groups) demanding achievers pay 'their fair share'. However, the achiever will try to mitigate the loss by spending less future time on production or trying to evade the confiscation in some other manner.

In most societies the hostile group will be the non-achievers or their representatives. And, depending on the extent of the hostility, deference and some sharing (by paying high taxes or making charitable contributions) is prudent! However, since the achiever doesn't want to relinquish a disproportionate share of his production, he will do everything possible to avoid that circumstance (tax evasion and production cuts are very probable outcomes).

In a democratic system, the process (taxation and regulation) causing unwanted sharing is likely to become excessive and detrimental to production since the non-achievers, representing the majority of voters, can exert political power over the achievers. American democracy did not accommodate total rule of the masses through most of it history. Up until 1930, the governmental control over citizens' incomes was modest and therefore wealth equality couldn't be dictated by the underachievers even though they represented the majority of voters. America's Constitution and Bill of Rights had been drafted by men who dreaded governmental interference in their private, public and business affairs.

Both achievers and non-achievers were convinced that freedom was better than governmental control. And, the idea of wealth sharing was deemed ridiculous. So, for about 150 years, the democratic process didn't work against the achievers. The Great Depression and the policies of President Franklin Roosevelt changed this.

Times were so bad that the American people turned to a leader who promised to change things for the better. By enacting governmental work programs and other welfare programs such as free food programs, the suffering of those out of work was mitigated to a certain extent. Although there is debate as to whether these governmental actions were the most appropriate, they achieved a floor for the suffering level of those out of work. Unfortunately, the American people relinquished a part of their independence in exchange for the government taking care of them. This crack in the American philosophy to keep government out of people's affairs has allowed the politicians to pry for even larger cracks in order to cater to America's non-achievers. Dependence on the government was no longer 100% unacceptable in society's mind. The reasons for dependency would grow over time and finally in 1964, President Lyndon Johnson's 'Great Society' made the crack a chasm by implementing policy based on a premise that non-achievement was the result of a concerted effort by the achievers to maintain the status quo of the non-achiever.

Since then, instead of the government being the enemy of the people as in the eyes of our forefathers, the achievers became the enemy of the people in the eyes of society.

The politicians had moved the country into a position to be controlled by the non-achievers. The democratic process and the fact that non-achievers represent a greater proportion of the populace would assure that outcome. The process would take time as the majority of the population was doing well as achievers boosted the economy. The seeds of this new philosophy however were sprouting everywhere. Hostile political organizations representing non-achievers were organizing and growing. And, their demands were starting to echo everywhere. Politicians were listening and enacting hundreds of new regulatory laws and new taxation policies.

Coercion of the achievers to share became a bigger part of the law. It had also become a socially accepted brain washing practice. In spite of society's brain washing, achievers never changed to like or want to share. They also never liked the government telling them what they could or couldn't do. They were no different in that respect than the non-achievers.

If hassle and the demand for sharing are moderate, the achiever will continue to produce (although at a modified pace). As the scale of each increases, his production will correspondingly decrease and may even put him in the category of non-achiever. What started out as moderate demands of the non-achiever in the 1960s became more aggressive over the next 50 years. America has reached the stage that with 50% of the population receiving some kind of government payout, many achievers have decided to become non-achievers.

Government dependence programs have reduced the incentive to work and in many cases made it unprofitable to work. So, achievers have become non-achievers. Now as the rank and file of the achievers diminishes, there is an increasing burden on those remaining to fill the gap. President Obama and the Democratic Party keep asking these individuals to give just a 'little more'. The 'little more' disincentive will drive more achievers to become non-achievers perpetuating the downward pressure on production in the economy. With over 11 million workers unemployed and much more underemployed in America, hasn't the policy to accommodate the non-achiever been the wrong policy!

50 years of programs to share the wealth, since President Johnson, have lead America to the brink of insolvency with the government owing $17 trillion! And, still the cry from the media and educators is the non-achiever is not getting enough! These intellects have forgotten that the achievers' response to an increasingly hostile environment (additional confiscation by the government) will result in the human behavior of shielding against this threat. That's why 50% of the population have moved toward the non-achiever status.

The socialistic concept (of fairness) that sharing wealth for the community's benefit will create a harmonious society is totally unrealistic and unworkable. The socialistic idea that most people are unselfish and would rather promote more equality in wealth by donating a portion of their assets versus being mostly self-interested has no supporting empirical evidence. By actively advocating this core element of socialism, educators and media have helped move America closer to a socialistic system where the government takes from the achievers to give to the non-achievers. With government controlling 40% of economic spending in the country, the socialistic policies of the last 80 years are strangling the country.

You liberals, don't you think you should look over the economic cliff's edge before you commit to pushing America over it by the continued insistence on your failed philosophy?!!!

DISCUSSION POINT 5
The Common Good Outweighs Individual Benefits?

Socialists argue that capitalism promotes only self-interest whereas socialism promotes the common good. Therefore socialism is a better system than capitalism.

The idea of common good can be easily be characterized as looking out for your neighbor. This idea has existed since the beginning of time as this practice was done for the 'common good' especially in troubled times. It arose out of neighbors looking out for each other when it was a necessity for survival. Reciprocal sharing, as a part of survival, meant that each party would help the other if needed and the favor would be returned in the future. Reciprocal sharing was not a one sided affair of always giving while the other side was always taking. In fact, the thought 'you owe me' was always present in historical times as well as today!

The socialistic philosophy eliminates the 'I owe you' from the concept of sharing. The non-achievers receive benefits from society regardless of a reciprocal contribution. You might say the behavior advocated by the church is the same behavior advocated by socialism - 'giving is as good as receiving' and 'each side gets equal benefit'. Who among the liberals practices that act of giving?! In the past, salvation of the average man's soul compelled him to give 10% of his income to the church to help his fellow man. The rich members of the church could have afforded much more but it was against their nature to give more so the church only asked for what they thought they could receive! Giving for the common good when combined with the reward of salvation weren't compelling reasons to share a significant portion of one's wealth in the past!

Self-interest has dominated human behavior since the beginning of time. Isn't it better to be ruled by a system, the capitalistic system, that adheres to natural behavior than to be ruled by one, socialism, that doesn't? Has human nature really changed in the last 50 years to make liberals think they can pass off the idea of substantial 'sharing' as workable because it is for society's common good. I think not!

DISCUSSION POINT 6
The Answer to Happiness – Wealth Equality or Freedom?

Socialist argue that the wealth gap between the 'rich' and the 'poor' is unfair and causes much of the unhappiness in society. They argue that the government must therefore be empowered to rectify this inequity. They believe that the narrower the gap, the happier society will become. This argument presupposes that other factors, either individually or jointly, do not play a larger role in the happiness of society's citizens. Although jealousy (envy of other man's economic status) is the powerful human emotion that can be attributed to the socialist's argument, it is hardly the driving force of human happiness.

Socialists would be well advised to take a course in human psychology to better understand the fallacy of this underpinning assumption in their philosophy. In fact, the United States of America was founded on the premise that freedom and the freedom to pursue happiness without government intervention was the most powerful motivator of human happiness.

The veracity of this premise is that the U.S. has achieved the status of being the most powerful, most wealthy country in the world. And, for well over 200 years, migration to the US has been unstoppable. The 'American Dream' is to build a better life for yourself and your family and has nothing to do with equal distribution of wealth. The fact that millions have come to America in spite of a massive gap between the rich and the poor pokes a huge hole in the argument for wealth equality.

The concept that wealth inequality creates tension in society is true. However, it is the thought process of jealous people that turns wealth inequality into the unfair category. Jealousy is a powerful human characteristic that needs a reason to justify the emotion. The socialistic politician provides that reason with the notion that the rich stole their wealth from the poor (by paying unfairly low wages to accumulate their wealth). This type of politician also criticizes the rich as selfishness and uncaring to create an even more powerful negative image of the rich to further promote jealousy and class warfare.

CHAPTER 6

However, selfishness is a very powerful human characteristic common to all men, not just the rich. The socialist's idea that the world would be a better place if there was more equality and sharing might be true. However, this would require mankind to change its nature. All humans are selfish and jealous (except possibly for saints). And, changing these characteristic of mankind is beyond the scope and capability of government (even if the government was run by saints - the few who aren't selfish and jealous).

The selfishness and jealousy in man is evidenced by observing everyday life or just taking note of every individual's own behavior. In order to capture followers, socialists must inflame human emotions to promote societal conflict in order to overpower rational thinking. The fact that the socialistic argument for wealth equality requires increasing conflict in society is another negative factor against it.

There are many socialistic talking points exclaiming the virtues of wealth equality. Most people want to achieve perfection in themselves and society. They perceive the perfect world to be one where everyone is happy. They see equality as a necessity for happiness as comparing status in their current life is a major element of their current happiness or unhappiness. Unfortunately, God did not create a perfect world of equality. Instead, he created a Darwinian world. And, in that world, wealth equality does not lead to the greatest satisfaction of mankind. And, attempts to achieve the ultimate wealth equality have historically only produced massive suffering. Happiness has been greatest in the American way of life that promotes freedom for the individual to do what he wants.

Discussion Point 7
Government vs. Capitalistic Rule of the Economy

The current claim of the liberals and the socialistic Democratic Party today is that the government is able to create social and economic policy that is more beneficial to society than the capitalistic system. They believe that a small group of elite politicians is better at understanding the needs of the public than the capitalistic market place where the interaction of millions of entrepreneurs and customers (determined solely by self-interest) determine individual happiness and also production.

Socialism was first proposed in the 19th century by Karl Marx. He stipulated that the general population would be better off if a socialistic system was put in place to more equally distribute a country's wealth. His theory was put in practice in a number of diverse countries in Europe, Russia, and China. After close to 100 years of these political systems being in place, the for-profit system in the U.S. has provided a standard of living many times higher for the general population than that achieved by those socialistic systems. (The standard of living in Russia is less than 1/5th the standard of living in the U.S. And, the standard of living in China is less than 1/10th the standard of living in the U.S.)

In addition to a higher standard of living, the for-profit system allows for less governmental interference in its citizens' lives. Socialistic systems require a myriad of rules, regulation and enforcement in how goods and services will be redistributed between producers and consumers in order to insure a semblance of providing the individual with his fair or equal share of production.

Also, risk taking behavior; in business (ex. - developing a new product), in recreation (ex. - extreme sports), in food consumption (enjoying salty and sugary foods that increase the chances of diabetes and heart disease), and in an infinite number of other areas; is likely to result in draining society's resources in the event of business failure, traumatic injury, health issues, and other costly issues. Therefore the socialistic system must attempt to prevent this type of activity as it would be unfair for the rest of society to have to subsidize the cost associated with risk taking behavior (New York city's Mayor Bloomberg has proposed rules to regulate the sale of 32 ounce sodas because the huge sugar intake is unhealthy and likely to lead to diabetes thereby putting a burden on the city's health system).

A capitalistic society does not have the above mentioned burden of regulating peoples' lives in an attempt to maintain the equality of consumption among its citizens. This additional freedom in a capitalistic society adds to the increased sense of wellbeing in for-profit societies vs. socialistic societies. The concept that a socialistic society is better suited for the happiness of its citizens is false for the reasons cited above.

DISCUSSION POINT 8
Profit Only Serves The Rich?

Socialists will make the argument that since Government is a non-profit entity, the transfer of commerce to it from a for-profit entity will result in at least the same quantity and quality of goods being produced. And, without unearned wealth (profit) being unfairly distributed to the capitalist more goods would be available to the workers. Therefore, the socialistic argument is that capitalism provides no benefits to society as the government can reproduce (quantity and quality) the goods and services of a capitalistic society without giving a piece to the business owner.

There are an overwhelming number of examples in America of the fallacy of that argument. The comparison between the services and costs of the U.S. Post Office and that of Federal Express might be one of the best examples. Post Office prices are much higher than those of Federal Express. In addition, the Post Office doesn't offer as many services as Federal Express. This is in spite of the fact that the Post Office had a monopoly on U.S. mail deliveries for over 150 years (And, the Post Office is also operating at a huge loss every year while Federal Express is extremely profitable). In fact, in spite of the private industry's profit margin, every business run by the private sector that competes against government service is much more cost effective.

The difference in the incentive program in private industry is so much greater than in the government that it creates a much more productive work environment in regard to innovation and hard work (Owners and employees will work harder and create better ways of doing tasks if they are rewarded through higher profits or higher pay). The resulting increase in productivity allows owners to take a share of the production while still having more product than would be available if run by a non-profit government entity (Government is structured to benefit those who follow the rules, not those who are innovative. Therefore workers who try to change the system of doing things to increase productivity are not significantly rewarded for success. In fact in many cases, their fellow workers feel threatened if one individual's productivity increases above the mean as superiors will question the work ethic of the fellow workers).

Worker incentive is at the heart of the capitalistic system. Worker incentive and wealth equality are diametrically opposed. Worker incentive means direct participation in a share of the wealth the worker creates. Wealth equality means an equal share of the wealth produced by all workers regardless of the difference in the amount of contribution. Lazy or unskilled workers receive similar amounts as the more productive. It is quite obvious that incentive drives human behavior and therefore the socialist's argument that the distribution of profit reduces the goods available for the worker is totally fallacious. In fact, the profit incentive creates more goods for both the profiteer and the worker.

DISCUSSION POINT 9
Administration of Rules Lowers Efficiency

Another argument against governmental control of wealth distribution concerns the inefficiencies caused by this societal system. The socialistic system requires that distributions be made according to governmental rules which are enforced by governmental bureaucracies. In the more socialistic countries, larger portions of the country's wealth need to be distributed. This requires a larger governmental bureaucracy which is needed to run its larger programs of regulation and redistribution. Aside from the lack of employee incentives to create efficient programs, the resources drained away, to support the bureaucracy, from producing tangible economic product make the socialistic system grossly inefficient. So, not only does the practice of wealth equality reduce the achievers incentive to work but it also creates more inefficiency by causing resources to be allocated to the non-productive task of administering programs of reallocation instead of programs that increase production.

DISCUSSION POINT 10
Capitalistic vs. Governmental Corruption

Socialists believe that a society run by the government is less corrupt than a society run by capitalism. The assumption made by this socialist argument is that the politicians who run the government for the 'benefit' of the public aren't as corrupt as the businessmen who run corporations for only their benefit and that of the owners. This assumption is ludicrous as all people are made from the same mold. Power corrupts regardless of the entity from which it emanates. As government is more powerful than any single business, corruption is greater in government than business. Abuse of power has never been reserved in its application.

In every political or economic structure, self-interest causes those with power to use it to their advantage. (In some cases, what is thought as abuse of power is actually usurpation of power. In any case, when the majority of citizens in a society feel unfairly treated by a power structure, this power structure can be considered abusive.) The larger any organization, (religious, political or economic), the greater is the inherent power of that organization. And, if the organization has a hierarchal leadership structure, then all the power of the organization resides in its small leadership.

The Government is the largest entity in the U.S. The Federal budget is $3.4T while the city, county, and state budgets total around another $3T. At the Federal level, 536 individuals, the Senators, the House Representatives, and the President, all have a say in how the budget will be spent. If the budget were divided equally among these members, each would control over $6B in yearly spending decisions. This tremendous power would even tempt the most honest individual to use his influence to better himself. Although there is a litany of rules against abuse of their political positions, somehow all these politicians become multi-millionaires either while in office or shortly thereafter. Their salaries as politicians don't account for their drastic increase in wealth (ex. - President Clinton has earned $90M since he left office in 1998.)! Could it be that these politicians are as self-interested as the elite businessman?

Corruption is the abuse of power. So, the question as to which system is more corrupt than the other can be addressed by understanding the power structure of each system. In a true Adam Smith capitalistic system, the free market determines the power structure. The entrepreneur has to conform to the free market otherwise he will go out of business. The Adam Smith scenario envisions competition to thwart the accumulation of power. However, in the real world, successful businesses when combined with leveraging politics have resulted in very powerful businesses being created. The power associated with these big businesses has often resulted in corruption.

However, governments have always had more power than any single one business. And, government is a hierarchal structure where the most power is concentrated in the upper echelon. Since socialism's concept relies on government taking care of its citizens in all aspects of their lives, its power structure is many times greater than that of a capitalistic orientated political structure. Therefore, since concentrated power produces the most corruption, it follows that a socialist government is much more corrupt than a capitalistic run government. And, a historical review of government structures reveals that to be the case.

DISCUSSION POINT 11
Capitalists Take Advantage of the Working Man?

A socialistic argument often starts with the premise that since maximizing profits is the sole motivation of capitalism, capitalists have no interest in the common wellbeing of society which requires attention to other factors (ex.- charity, decent wages, respect for fellow men, etc.). And, socialists argue that the worker is at the mercy of the capitalist. Therefore, capitalism is an anti-social, evil concept. Socialists point to the plight of the worker all through the Industrial Revolution as well as the gap between the rich and the poor today to make their point (Protecting workers from the negative effects of low wages and poor working conditions, etc. created by totally self-interested powerful businessmen plays well on the sympathetic ears of the public as workers represent a much larger portion of society than entrepreneurs).

The missing part of the socialistic argument is that a capitalistic society opens opportunity for every member of society. The hard worker and the entrepreneur coming from all types of backgrounds are presented with opportunities to better their lives. Both successful risk taking and the hard work ethic are rewarded with either financial rewards or social advancement or both. Successful risk takers are usually more successful than the hard worker and therefore are the individuals most able to move up society's social ladder to the elite level. And, political power can be obtained through the economic influence gained by the risk taker. By promoting hard work and risk taking, the capitalistic society is constantly increasing productivity, social mobility and the standard of living of the people living in that society.

By encouraging new risk taking ideas that lead to more productivity, the power of the human brain is unleashed to create powerful economic growth. Although society benefits greatly with each successful new idea, each corresponding risk taker's benefits are astronomical in comparison to the average individual's growth in wealth from the new idea (when a new product benefits millions of people, even taking a tiny piece of the total benefit creates huge returns for the entrepreneur). This is a major cause in the disparity of wealth between rich and poor, not stealing from, taking advantage of or abusing the worker.

New more productive systems do have short-term negative economic effects. They cause economic displacement. Old jobs are no longer needed and workers need to learn new skills to be valuable (worker displacement during the Industrial Revolution led to the rise in the idea of socialism). This period of displacement also widens the wealth gap between the rich and the poor (even if just on a short-term basis). Social unrest occurs as workers lose jobs and also their accustomed standard of living while the capitalist benefits. This scenario causes socialists to find evil in the capitalistic system (The rich are portrayed as evil because they 'don't care' about the people 'they' put out of work). And, if the disparity of wealth increases over time, the power structure of society also changes.

If the new systems put in place create a huge increase in productivity, the risk taker's enterprise will grow rapidly and gain huge economic and political power. If left unfettered, this power will at some point become corrupt. Socialists attribute this extreme evil of unfetter power to the capitalistic system when in fact the same corruption of power occurs even more often in aristocracies and other political systems (Unfettered capitalism, in the early 1900's, in the new industries of steel and oil led to massive corporations who used their power unfairly. The Sherman Anti-Trust Act was passed to dilute the power of the huge companies engaging in anti-competitive practices).

Instead of following a rational thinking process that economic progress (more efficient production) naturally will lead to social disruption (through workers put out of work needing to develop new skills), the socialist blames the capitalist for that negative outcome but doesn't credit the entrepreneur for society's overall economic gain (more productive capacity). Although the (distasteful) profit causes the eventual advancement (through increased production) in the wellbeing of society, socialists will never acknowledge this huge benefit of capitalism.

Successful new technologies often result in the rapid growth of companies causing the original entrepreneur to lose control of his company to professional business managers. These individuals are many times more interested in milking the new technology for their own benefit rather than in using the new profits to discover other more productive technologies. They use the power of the large asset base of the company for propaganda (marketing), negotiations (with workers and suppliers) and political agendas (lobbying) to enhance their own and the company's short-term profitability. Once company control is passed to professional business managers, unless the owners take an active role, those businesses lose much of their capitalistic characteristics which become replaced with many aspects of crony capitalism (Cronyism is defined as favoritism shown to friends without regard to their qualifications as in helping them gain positions they are unworthy of).

Entrepreneurs seeking long-term profitability require the most efficient systems in order to achieve it. Professional business managers who don't have an ownership stake in the company except through stock options are much less concerned with optimal long-term profitability. In the short-run, the anti-competitive actions described above by professional managers help fend off the competition of newer, more productive ideas. In the long-run, these large companies fail as increasingly productive ideas from smaller entrepreneurial companies take market share from anti-competitive less efficient larger companies.

Crony capitalism leads to failure. Socialists lump companies with professional businesses managers (crony capitalism) together with true capitalism (entrepreneurial managed businesses) and cite the injustices of crony capitalism to indict the true capitalistic system (A current example is the 2008 housing bubble where professional business managers put in place a massive risk taking process that entrepreneurs would never have initiated. The owners or shareholders of the large banks lost most of their equity while the managers - CEOs, etc., - made millions before the collapse and lost nothing after). The portrayal of crony capitalism as true capitalism is another major error in the socialist's argument about the evils of capitalism.

When one views the history of capitalism in the western world, it has shown that a constantly changing economic and political hierarchy takes place under that system. As huge businesses rise and fall, so does their economic power and political influence. And, although change (caused by better technology) in the business environment causes economic disruptions (recessions and depressions), the benefit of the economic progress (more production by more efficient means) has resulted social and economic mobility for the working man. It has also resulted in the massive improvement of the standard of living in the western world in the last 200 years. In western society, the poor are living many times better than the aristocracy of the 1800s. The average man has taken advantage of the capitalistic system, not vice-versa.

DISCUSSION POINT 12
Modern Free Markets Have Failed?

Leading members (Hillary Clinton in a speech on 6/4/2007, President Obama's 2008 and 2012 campaign message) of the socialistic Democratic Party have stated that the free market has failed and therefore government is needed to replace the failed capitalistic system. These socialists attribute the Great Recession to a unfettered corrupt capitalistic system. They blame the financial institutions - the banks, the brokerage houses, the mortgage companies, etc. - for deceiving ignorant home buyers about the affordability of their actions. They claim the magnitude and scope of this deception caused the housing bubble, its demise and the ensuing financial crisis.

However, it was governmental policy, at the time, to encourage as much home ownership in the nation as possible. Lending standards were eased for Fannie Mae and Freddie Mac, two gigantic government-sponsored mortgage lending entities. Fannie Mae and Freddie Mac were allowed and encouraged to guarantee loans created for Mortgage Backed Securities. This created tremendous liquidity in the mortgage lending market and was a major stimulus in the 'housing bubble'.

The financial crisis that occurred with the meltdown of the housing market was a result of bad government policy (helped by lobbyists) , bad corporate policy (greed by the C - level executives) and the greed of the public. Greed at every level was indeed the cause of the 2008 economic meltdown. However, the lending standards of private industry became so ridiculously low that any true (greedy) capitalist would never have considered risking his capital. Instead, the corporate managers with none of their own money at risk but lots of potential reward with their stock options proceeded to make risky loans on behalf of their shareholders anyhow. Politicians were interested in helping the building industry and were inspired by their lobbyists. They also knew a robust housing market was good for their re-election chances. So, they chose to ignore the fact that irresponsible lending standards would lead to major problems in the future. When the inevitable came to pass, these same politicians chose to deny complicity and instead chose to use the crisis to increase their power.

Politicians will never let a crisis go to waste. And, the financial crisis was the perfect example of a political power grab that led to instituting more regulations. Passage of the Dodd-Frank Act was the result.

On another front, the excuse of failure of the free market in healthcare insurance is also being used as the political reason for the power grab of Obamacare. Because the healthcare insurance industry is so closely tied to the healthcare industry (it negotiates and pays most of the nations bills concerning healthcare), this is really a political power grab to control all of the American healthcare industry which represents 18% of the GDP of the nation! Politicians blamed the healthcare insurers 1) for discriminating against people with pre-existing conditions, 2) for having policies that were unaffordable for 48 million Americans, 3) for kicking the insured off their policies when they were needed the most, and 4) for not allowing the insured to move their policies from job to job or state to state. Private health insurance needed to be replaced because of these failures, according to Democratic politicians, by the current Obamacare law. Let's examine whether the 'failure' of private healthcare insurance justifies the creation of another massive governmental bureaucracy.

The Obamacare law has created 20,000 pages of new regulations. In order to comply with this massive amount of new regulations, the healthcare industry will incur much additional costs in changing the way it does business. Future costs will also be significantly increased by the added cost of compliance with thousands of new rules. In addition, the government will incur significant costs in the way of auditing, monitoring, and enforcing the added rules in the new law. On top of these added costs, as Obamacare takes on the role of the biggest national healthcare insurer in a business it knows nothing about, it assumes the risk of spending substantial amounts of tax-payer dollars if premiums collected do not cover the added expenses of the program. The current estimated additional cost of

Obamacare is between $1.3 trillion and $3 trillion over the next 10 years.

Problems in government management of this healthcare program can already be seen in the poor development of its website and the massive cost overrun of this IT project. The chief architect of Obamacare, Dr. Ezekiel Emanuel, stated that the work for the website only required simple basic programming. His analogy was the block and tackling of a football game, not the strategy. One must think that if the easiest part of government execution results in long delays and massive cost overruns, what should be expected when the difficult strategies need to be implemented! What might cause other healthcare expenses to go up under Obamacare, aside from the general poor management skills of government?

1. Statistics show that individuals, as a group, with pre-existing conditions require substantially more treatment than the general population. Insurance companies have factored the increased cost of this treatment into the higher rates they charge for these conditions. Generally insurable pre-existing conditions refer to genetics or current physical attributes that are more likely to result in future health care needs. For insurance purposes a pre-existing condition is not a healthcare issue that requires immediate therapy (Ex. - A genetic condition that shows cancer is twice as likely to occur in those with the condition vs. those without is a pre-existing condi-

tion. An individual who already has cancer is considered sick, not having a pre-existing condition.). In a number of pre-existing conditions, the future expected cost is extremely high. In order to profitably insure this condition, the insurance rates have to also be extremely high. Most individuals can't afford these high rates so insurance companies don't offer policies. Obamacare plans to cover these individuals. It is estimated that 2 to 4 million Americans with pre-existing conditions do not have insurance. Analysis of current State plans that cover some high-risk individuals indicate that with rates 50% to 100% over normal insurance rates, subsidies of over $4 thousand an individual are required to keep those plans viable. An article in National Affairs estimates the subsidized cost of insuring pre-existing individuals to be around $16 billion a year if they paid 150% to 200% of normal insurance rates. *(http://www.nationalaffairs.com/publications/detail/ how-to-cover-pre-existing-conditions)*

2. 48 million Americans do not have healthcare insurance. Either they don't have the money to pay for it or they don't believe it is in their best interests to pay for it because in many cases it is free (emergency rooms cannot refuse non-paying patients). A profit hungry insurance industry surely would have liked to enroll 48 million more people as customers if they thought it profitable. Since they are without

plans, they must have been considered unprofitable potential customers. Obamacare's goal is to enroll these 48 million uninsured and make them pay something for their insurance. Since the penalty for not becoming enrolled is somewhere between $95 and $2085 per year (see link below), and the current cost of healthcare insurance generally runs between $2500/yr. (healthy and young) to $12000/yr. (somewhat healthy but old), it is likely that the healthy will choose to pay a penalty because they still will be able to receive treatment by enrolling when they are sick. If the healthcare insurance industry thought this was a profitable approach to gain 48 million more customers, undoubtedly they would have taken it. The government's approach to insuring these individuals will be very costly. An added cost of $1000/year will mean tax-payers will need to foot another $48 billion/year. *http://www.forbes.com/sites/mikepatton/2013/10/28/obamacare-penalties-and-exemptions/*

3. This problem of people losing health insurance is a glitch in the mechanics of the current health insurance industry. Legislating liability for mistakes that result in insurance policy cancellation would immediately fix the problem. And, extending the the life of Cobra coverage past 18 months would be an additional fix. A small bill vs. massive legislation certainly would be the better approach.

Currently, insurance companies cannot kick their paying customers off their plan for no reason. Problems emanating from COBRA plans may lead to the insured losing his plan. The COBRA insured continue to use their former employers plan after they leave the company. If their former company fails, the insurance plan the company had is no longer in existence and therefore there is no entity plan to be attached to. Also, for plans still in existence, the COBRA insured pays a third party administrator of the plan who is then responsible for writing a new check to the insurance company. Errors on the part of the administrator can result in the insurance company not being paid and the cancellation of the policy.

4. This is another problem that could be fixed easily if the politicians in each state decided to relinquish their power associated with State healthcare law for the benefit of the people. Currently, interstate health insurance is prohibited by law. Each state has different rules concerning health insurance and none of them want to give up their power concerning this industry. This problem is falsely presented as a problem with private insurance.

A synopsis of the 4 problems causing politicians to criticize the current healthcare insurance industry have nothing to do with the bad management or the evil outcomes of a profit motivated industry. In order to solve the main two issues, pre-existing conditions and the uninsured, major funding will be required. Instead of being honest with the American people and telling them the estimated cost of this funding, Democratic politicians have chosen to implement a law with 20,000 pages of new regulations and to tell the public their new government run plan won't cost the tax-payer anything! When every other government run organization can't compete with private industry, this position is incredibly untruthful and unrealistic.

Whenever there is a crisis in the economy, socialists revert back to the propaganda that capitalism is a failure and the ensuing suffering and problems of the general public have been caused by the greed and corruption in the ranks of the capitalists. This position is no different now than the socialistic argument starting in the 1800s and now continuing into the 21st century! Each pronouncement of failure over this 200 year period has been wrong (as the standard of living in capitalistic countries has soared) in spite of the normal amount of corruption (inherent in every large organization including government) found in the capitalistic system.

Economic systems have cycles just as people have their ups and downs. If an economic system has delivered continuous success in the past, short-term negative fluctuations and new problems arising out of past successes should not be recognized as proof of failure. Today's politicians who are advocating for this type of policy are just trying to create power for themselves. And, they are exposing society to great risk.

DISCUSSION POINT 13
Capitalism Inspires, Socialism Decays

Capitalism promotes economic growth by creating a competitive system that encourages individuals to work for a better life in terms of economic product and health matters. Socialism, on the other hand, does not promote economic growth but instead promotes the concept of fairness and equality as a way to happiness. This policy necessarily causes economic stagnation if not economic decay.

Socialists make the presumption that, in general, individuals in society are more concerned with the wealth equality of society than with increasing their own wealth. It follows therefore that if any individual's personal wealth increases at a faster rate than society's, a disequilibrium will occur (the spread between the rich and the poor will increase), causing an unwanted condition in a socialistic society. Then in order for a socialistic society to increase the general wealth of the society without changing wealth distribution, it would be necessary to require all citizens to work harder as a group or become more productive by improving systems currently in place.

Problems are evident in either case that would and have historically prevented society's economic advancement in a socialistic system. If one presumes socialistic societies have a mandate from their citizens to increase production, then in the first case all working members of the socialistic society would have to agree to commensurately increase their workloads to ensure fairness and the maintenance of the wealth status quo of the system. Otherwise, the increase in the work load would be unevenly distributed and wealth distribution would change.

Mass acceptance will not occur because the task of getting a majority of people to agree on anything is hard enough let alone getting everyone to agree to reduce their leisure time without rules to punish those that didn't comply. Voting to sacrifice for the 'common good' only happens in the most dire circumstances. Therefore it would be impossible for a socialistic society to increase its standard of living by asking all its citizens to work harder.

In the second case, in order to improve systems or productivity requires ingenuity and risk taking (attempting a new untried process). As mentioned before, neither attribute is highly regarded in a socialistic society. The learning by trial and error exposes the socialistic society to a possible loss of wealth. And, there is no gauge to accurately evaluate the likelihood of success or failure. Only new projects that received the consensus of a socialistic committee would have a chance of being funded. And, history shows that successful entrepreneurs build businesses counter to accepted beliefs. Therefore, the culture of socialism will prevent the improvement in productivity because approval of successful new different methods to improve systems will not happen. The underlying assumption that maintenance of wealth equality is essential to happiness in the socialistic system ensures at best there is no wealth growth in the purely socialistic system. The historical outcome of socialistic societies is one of not only no growth but decay.

CHAPTER 6

DISCUSSION POINT 14 -
Hypocrisy - Liberal Philosophy vs. Liberal Behavior

Liberals will surely argue that the selfish behavior of the elite in history was deplorable (most wealth was owned by the aristocracy and wars were provoked by these elite to rearrange the aristocratic hierarchy). Some liberals attribute the elitist behavior to the poor economic environment of the past. However, now that worldly goods are plentiful, it's time for the elite to become more civilized and share their wealth (It is very interesting to note that the sharing the wealth concept is only openly promoted in the developed world, not in the under-developed or developing world).

One would assume, based on the liberal ideology, that mankind is good, generous, and unselfish. Since liberal ideas believe selfishness is bad and sharing and forgiveness are good, one might think that the liberal's value system was a product of their childhood experience where they experienced sharing and forgiveness and were happy because of it.

These individuals must have grown up in the ideal family where there was no conflict for attention, resources, or differing ideas, and where the workload of household duties, chores, and bringing in the bucks was shared happily by family members. And, each member of the family had no jealousy about another's looks, intellectual or athletic abilities, or social skills. And, there were no sibling or parental preferences that created ill feelings. In addition to the perfect family setting, it might also be assumed that these liberals must have also grown up in perfect social settings also. If somehow, an unfortunate incident occurred such as being bullied, being criticized, being called a loser in sports, or just running into the wrong person, these liberals would have excused these actions by believing that they were outlier events and that the people involved could be changed for the better. Although, these events would be unpleasant, the liberal would never carry a grudge or seek revenge even if only in his mind.

If the liberal mindset is not based on an experience of sharing and forgiveness but based on a perception that childhood life would have been better if family and acquaintances would have been nicer (because they shared and forgave), then the liberal philosophy is dependent on dreams that utopia can exist if most people change their behavior. This dependence on the hope that mankind will change its characteristic of selfishness is a far cry from the liberal propaganda that blames only the few rich members of society for being selfish and being responsible for all that is unfair and wrong. The task of changing the behavior of a few seems within the realm of possibility. The task of changing the behavior of all of mankind would be viewing as an impossible task even by most liberals. So in order to retain their liberal outlook, these individuals must ignore actual human behavior to fool themselves.

Core elements of the liberal's belief system are as follows. Liberals articulate their belief that love triumphs over hardship. They say they believe that peace triumphs over individual needs for worldly goods. They insinuate that people are more interested in the welfare of those around them than in their own welfare. They publish the belief that if someone has different values than their own, somehow society is at fault. And, somehow that fault must have been unintentional since most people in society want the best for each other. They believe that competition in any field should be filled with comradery without motive to show oneself better or to gain reward.

With this liberal belief system in mind, it would be informative to determine whether the life styles of leading liberals conform to their espoused belief system. The current leading list of liberals includes movie stars, wealthy financiers, wealthy politicians and wealthy business men. And, of course there is Mother Theresa. I would assume that with a common belief system, they would all share equally and have all lived their lives with as much consideration for those less privileged as themselves.

Take a hard look at the facts. Need I say more? Do liberals lead double lives, one advocating the politics inspired by their idealistic views while the other harshly competing in the real world? If this elite list of liberals care so much about the inequality of means in the world, then why don't they share enough of their wealth with those in need to bring about an equal means status, including their own, to all they help.

As an example, if this elite group as a whole or individually thought an income of $200K/year was an appropriate sharing income level, and their level of income was $2M/year, then these individuals should give away $1.8M/year. This amount could then be divided among individuals earn-ing less to supplement their incomes to a level of $200K. So, instead of complaining about inequality while owning multiple million dollars houses, flying private jets, vacationing at $1000+ per night resorts, throwing $1M+ parties, drinking $1000 bottles of wine, and buying $1M+ pieces of jewelry and art, they should act out their advocacy and give away that which makes their economic circumstances so disparate from their fellow man.

In regard to the liberals' attitude to treat everyone respectfully as equal brothers in the human race, here again there is a massive contrast in the ideology espoused and the actions taken in the real world. Most movie stars are extremely arrogant people. They expect to be pampered by everyone they touch including all members of their production crews. Most don't have respect for their families as they are constantly changing partners and usually have little time for their children. As a group, their private and work lifestyle does not live up to their ideology.

The wealthy corporate raiders or financiers who consider themselves to be liberal, like George Soros, have little social conscience also. They don't care if their financial transactions disrupt economies or sovereign nations. Their jobs also force them to revamp companies by firing unproductive workers without pre-arranging new jobs for them.

The next group, the wealthy business men also aren't affected by their political bend in their business dealings. Their job forces them to be as competitive and to make as much profit as possible. Workers' salaries are not equal and business protocol requires subservience to the bosses. In addition, when inefficient competitors are put out of business, there is no mourning for the workers put out of work or the capital loss inflected on the owners. The successful businessman is one whose job is to destroy less competitive businesses. To be competitive, he is willing to step on anyone and everything in the path to success. Steve Jobs is a prime example of the successful businessman. He had no concern about doing whatever it took to make Apple the great success. In the business world, the successful businessman needs to compete with low prices and good service. He needs to fire the incompetent and those lacking in business and social skills in order to compete. Yet, these same people voice concern over the wellbeing of the worker in their ideology.

Finally, let's look at the wealthy liberal politicians' treatment of their fellow man. In the elections just run (2012), the liberal politicians labeled the conservatives as women haters, racists, war mongers, and wealthy robber barons. The running of this campaign was in direct contrast with those equalitarian and brotherly love views espoused by their utopian liberal view of mankind. The nation's conservatives represent over 40% of the voting public. So if the liberals actually believe that man is a benevolent species, and therefore would live according to an idealists philosophy, how can they be reconciled to the fact that over 40% of the population supports leaders that don't share that viewpoint and that their own political leaders (who must also be benevolent) didn't have a second thought before unmercilessly attacking conservatives and their agenda.

The lifestyles of the rich and famous liberals are contradictory to their philosophy and their talking points. In reality, they are just hypocritical snake oil salesmen. When they start to act like Mother Teresa, only then should the world listen and respect them. Until then, the economic, social and political policies that these people will try to put in place will lead to disaster. Policies based on the erroneous assumption that self-interest is evil and must be controlled by government has led to the growth of unified power in government, big business, and big unions. To arrive at fairness to all, the liberals will aspire to use more regulation and taxation to insure their view of society comes to pass. This will lead to more growth in government along with massive power. And, as we all know, power corrupts. And absolute power corrupts absolutely.

Many liberals are romantics. They are idealistic in their dreams if not in their personal behavior. Reality isn't what it is but what it should be. The leaders of this movement however are mainly power grabbers using the liberal illusion to achieve their political aspirations. Although, the liberal (socialistic) concept of creating fairness is totally disruptive and unworkable, these leaders continue to promote a deadly fairytale. And, unfortunately the main media outlets have fallen under this romantic spell. The liberal propaganda outlet has been unleashed to capture American minds. Our forefathers would be aghast at how Freedom of the Press is being used!!!

DISCUSSION POINT 15
The Perfect Socialistic Setting – The Family

Shouldn't socialism thrive in the family setting where all family members have the most interest in sharing and each other's happiness? The family is the most basic core of society. Assets held by a married couple are usually equally co-owned and liabilities are also equally shared. The children rely on the parents to provide for them and most likely will inherit the wealth created by their parents. There is expectation that all members of the family will look out for each other throughout their lives. This sounds like the perfect socialistic setting. One would think testing core socialistic assumptions in the family environment would likely verify their veracity. One would expect that sharing and happiness and no strife would be the dominant behavior if key socialistic assumptions about human attributes were true.

Divorce statistics show that today almost 50% of new marriages result in divorce. Even though sharing would be expected in a married couple, many times married couples deem the allocation of money unfair in respect to each parties' contribution to the family's wellbeing. Many divorces result from one of the spouses feeling unfairly treated in regard to money issues. And, siblings very rarely share wealth as adults. They consider what they earned on their own or inherited to be their own assets. If there is a large discrepancy in wealth among siblings (regardless of its origin), usually it causes tremendous damage to the relationships involved. Sharing is not natural so even in the family setting where it should thrive, it doesn't. The socialistic concepts that would be expected to flourish in a family environment don't work.

The self-interest and jealousy traits in humans are so dominate that even in the ideal environment, socialistic concepts don't work. In society, in general, where the individual has very little in common with his fellow man, what will give rise to the concept working better? Allocation of wealth as a fairness concept hasn't worked in any society. The capitalistic concept of allocation by achievement has built the most wealthy society in history where the poor live better than the kings of yesteryear.

CONCLUSION

The Discussion Points above have highlighted the key assumptions and arguments that are made by liberals advocating socialism. The main argument that emanates from the liberal is that a more altruistic social (economic and political) system would be better for mankind. Since most societies promote a Christian like moral philosophy (love thy neighbor, be honest and truthful, selfishness is bad, etc.), the socialistic philosophy would appear to have many positive merits. The arguments against socialism found in the above discussion points evaluates the real nature of man vs. the idealist nature in man. By assuming that the world operates on realism and not on idealistic assumptions, this chapter provides reasoning why large long-term experiments in socialism have failed and why capitalism is such a superior economic system.

The next two Chapters of this book will discuss the reason for socialism's growth in America and the consequences of that growth.

CHAPTER 7

Why Socialism Has Taken Hold In America

L et's talk about fairness in America and how the concept has evolved and is causing changes in our way of life. The post war economic boom that has lasted from 1950 to almost today created an American standard of living unseen in history. Advances in technology in all aspects of American business produced productivity gains that have allowed the work week to shrink from over 50 hours/week to less than 40 hours/week. It allowed the standard working man's vacation to go from 1 week a year to up to 6 weeks a year. Health care gains increased the average life span by almost 20 years. Automation in the household drastically reduced the burden of a housewife's physical labor. Automation in the workforce did the same thing for workers.

The economic boom created enough wealth for Americans to give their children a more optimistic view of life than they as parents were given. These children were the baby boomers. Their parents had grown up in a Great Depression where life was hard and the only way to provide for your family was to work hard most of the time. There was little time to be concerned about the social injustices of the country. The individual either pulled his own weight by providing for his family or he was considered an outcast and a blight on society. The determination of fair was whether the action was beneficial to society or detrimental. It was the fault of the individual if he didn't contribute enough to production to feed his family. If a man's failure resulted in society taking care of him and his family, this was unfair to society and was socially unacceptable.

However as the country prospered, this attitude changed. The country began producing a surplus of goods causing a change in the criteria that determined fairness. Increasingly, individual rights gained more importance in regard to fairness standards. The idea of fairness shifted to evaluating whether society was treating individuals and groups of individuals fairly not whether individuals were treating society fairly.

The Civil Rights Movement was the first major indication that society was shifting its views. This movement's acceptance was followed by the Women's Rights Movement along with the Sexual Revolution and the Gay Rights Movement. The importance of every individual was gaining momentum while the importance of institutions such as government and business was in decline. Previous wars such as World War II and the Korean War had been considered necessary in spite of the great economic and individual sacrifices that were made. Americans believed in these wars as necessary to maintain the great American way of life. Government had been trusted to make the right decisions to protect its citizens.

This trust evaporated with the baby boomers who had decided that individual rights were more important than societal rights determined by society's institutions. The Vietnam

War was viewed as an attack on not only individual American rights but also human rights everywhere. Killing for whatever reason was an egregious act. And, all those who supported killing had to be villains. Big business and all government institutions associated with war were part of that group. The massive increase in American wealth in the 1950's and the 1960's was allowing for the transformation of the idea of fairness. The majority of baby boomers had never lived in an atmosphere of need. Their lives were good and they expected them to get better. The continuing advancement of technology produced productivity gains that gratified their expectations. The increasing wealth of the times allowed the majority of baby boomers to think about those less fortunate. Why was there this big gap between the wealthy, the less fortunate and the average guy (or middle class)?

As social injustices had been addressed with the Civil Rights and other movements, a corresponding movement on the rights of the poor needed also to be addressed. The Great Society movement was promoted by President Lyndon Johnson and instituted by Congress. Individual rights and the liberal movement were marching forward hand in hand. The definition of fairness kept changing in the direction of individual rights and addressing the inequality of individuals in the society. The economy had created enough wealth to be spread around without truly negatively affecting the life style of the majority of citizens. So, as a way to be fair, American politicians created policies to spread the wealth.

Today, society is living with the fairness assumptions based on 60 years of massive economic progress. However, the economic consequences that these government policies created with a baby boomer fairness agenda need to be examined. An economic crisis has enveloped America. And, what is considered fair today may revert to unfair if America's economic situation turns for the worse. For almost 2/3rds of the 20th century, government played a minor role in society except in war.

Today, government represents almost 40% of U.S. GDP with almost 50% of Americans relying on varying degrees of payment transfers from the government. With the government budget deficit running close to 25% over tax receipts which is close to 10% of GDP, it appears society's generosity has overshot its ability to pay. With individuals believing in fairness standards currently at a 60 year peak in relation to society's rights, a conflict has developed between the ability to deliver goods and services and the expectation that there is enough available to fulfill the aspirations of the general population.

An insistence on taking care of the individual will result in demands for bigger government. A bigger government will require the appropriation of a larger share of GDP. As government does not produce goods or investment, a larger government expropriation of production will be a disincentive for achievers and will result in less production and less goods for everyone, not more. Also, the additional government reliance will result in a bigger more powerful governmental bureaucracy which will cling to secure jobs in an increasingly poor economic environment. Governmental employees will sacrifice their own freedom and that of others to protect their own livelihood by following the rules necessary to keep their jobs. History shows dictatorships grow out of this type of environment. When that happens individual rights become no longer important. Society's rights become the only important right and the elite government officials will be in control in the determination of those rights.

The irony of this possible cycle is that the massive productivity gains that led to unparalleled gains in freedom and wellbeing also created the atmosphere of entitlement which in turn could lead to a forfeiture of individual responsibility in favor of governmental responsibility and power. If the cycle runs its full course, Americans will have turned their backs on the productive powers of a free economy by giving power to unproductive government entities. And, in the process, they are likely to lose their freedom, all in the quest for a 'fairer society'.

The current Democratic Party's socialistic call for more fairness and equality is about expanding entitlement programs and more government. It's amazing that this socialistic attempt to achieve 'fairness' is likely to have such negative dramatic consequences.

CHAPTER 8

The Consequences of 80 Years of America's Liberal Policies

American socialism which started out in the 1930's as an attempt to help the common man has turned into a political two-party grab for ultimate power. Although early American capitalism lead to massively powerful large corporations that 'abused' their power, the current political power grab will have similar negative consequences to society.

In American history prior to 1930, the size of government was small in relation to the rest of the economy. The government's budget was 7% of GDP until 1920 when it approached 20%. Even though the government didn't influence the economy significantly through its spending, power resided in its ability to create legal regulation. Government regulation could therefore be used to mitigate the abuse of power of large organizations if it arose. In the case of large corporations in the early 1900s, many thought them to be too powerful. Regulation was then enacted to reduce their monopolistic power by breaking them apart. American society had shown its ability to keep in check the corporate power structure. Fortunately for American society, the American political system was structured to handle problems caused by big business while still not disturbing the process that created such massive economic wealth.

Government in America today has evolved into an extremely powerful force by not only being a regulatory body to prevent abuse of power but also by controlling the disposition of 40% of the country's production. Politicians have put the government in the position to not only prevent the abuse of private industry's power but also to dictate total economic policy for private industry. Included in this policy is determining acceptable profitability levels, hiring practices, product acceptability (what products are good and bad for the country), and liability issues. By becoming the major force in the economy, American government has vastly expanded its power in the last 80 years. Since government doesn't produce any physical product or new consumer services, Americans haven't benefited from any increased productivity due to this expansion. In fact, the expansion has reduced the resources available to its citizens because 40% of U.S. production is being used to support unproductive governmental activity.

Clearly, America's massive government has created a power structure ripe for monumental abuse. Politicians claim the benefits of this Big Government are; controlling the greed of the rich and powerful; controlling large corporations from abusing the environment, its workers, and the public; determining an educational agenda; controlling its citizens from carrying out socially unacceptable behavior; and, determining the acceptable level of income distribution.

Only two political parties control this power structure. And, a small leadership group of each party controls the agenda of each party. Governmental power is in the hands of only a few politicians. Americans, who didn't like the power exerted by large corporations in the early 1900s or don't like the power inherent in large corporations today, have allowed their government to become hundreds of times more powerful. In the process, Americans have made the power obtained from producing more goods (capitalism) much less than the power obtained from creating laws to redistribute (socialism) those goods. And, this change has resulted in a concentrated power structure controlled by a small political leadership group.

Americans have been convinced by political propaganda that the top priority of government is to look out for the interests of its citizens. This propaganda has stated that big business can't be trusted because its greedy profit incentive induces bad behavior. The propaganda neglects to discuss the fact that both big business and big government are run by people. And, all people are self-interested and will take advantage of every situation to benefit themselves. So, both executives in big business and political leaders in government will make decisions to benefit themselves.

The altruistic claims of politicians aren't true. Power corrupts them just as power corrupts everyone! And, absolute power corrupts absolutely. American government is approaching the absolute power stage. And, only a few elite politicians control the government. I ask the socialistic liberals, are you not students of history? Hasn't every concentrated power structure been corrupt? And, doesn't socialism advocate a concentrated power structure?

Many people are susceptible to con artists. Con artists are believable because they are well practiced at their art. They know peoples' weaknesses. And, they prey on them. Promises of rich monetary and emotional rewards are the propaganda used to lighten the wallet of their victims. The promises of politicians are very similar. Today's political inducements are to save the world from the polluters and global warming and to save the poor from the clutches of the rich. This heroic agenda has massive appeal especially when presented without the consequences of following the recommended actions or evaluating the truth of the assumptions that were made to determine that the stated problem actually existed.

Americans have fallen under the spell of the politicians for the past 80 years with promises starting with a social safety net for those out of work to promises of complete healthcare coverage. The early promises of security seemed to work out as the massive productivity of the American economy provided the excess product necessary for confiscation (taxes) to make politicians' proclamations look good. With early success creating more political power, more and more entitlement promises have been enacted that have caused additional confiscation and allowed power to flow to the politicians controlling the programs created. The fairy tale of getting something for nothing has temporarily become true for the American public.

Unfortunately, the real world exists. The giveaway programs have become too large and have caused the U.S. debt to become close to 100% of GDP. The tremendous growth in debt is an unmistakable marker that America can't afford its entitlement programs. Yet, politicians still hunger for more power and advocate for more free goods for the public. And,

THE CONSEQUENCES OF 80 YEARS
OF AMERICA'S LIBERAL POLICIES

Americans fortified by the 'success' of past programs believe America is still rich enough to give more.

The disclaimer required of sellers of investment products which states that "past success is not an indicator of future success" is being totally ignored by the public in American politics! Using the past 'success' of entitlement programs, the Democratic party is pushing for complete socialism and the public is sucking it all up. The con artists are winning which means disaster is waiting. This is the consequence of 60 years of American liberal policies!!!

CHAPTER 9

Mending The Broken American Dream

As Elvis' song Suspicious Minds states "we're caught in a trap"! Americans have fallen hook line and sinker into the politicians' trap that promises massive government spending programs will take care of all Americans. Politicians claim that most Americans only need to spend a little more in taxes to achieve these awards since the rich will provide most of the additionally needed funds to make these programs financially viable. The programs currently in operation promise retirement benefits (social security, etc.), unemployment benefits (unemployment insurance, etc.), comprehensive healthcare coverage (Obamacare, etc.), and extensive welfare plans (food stamps, section 8 housing, etc.). The massive burden of these extensive programs has caused the current government deficit of $17 trillion which is also expanding rapidly. Common sense leads to the conclusion that the political solution of just a 'little more tax' is grossly in error!

In spite of the fact that every private and government entity, that is expert at budget analysis, states that the current benefits associated with these programs will bankrupt the government, regardless of taxation policy for the rich, in the not too distant future, America's politicians still maintain their lie by refusing to discuss that likely outcome with the public (WSJ article by Chris Cox – former chairman of House Republican Party Policy Committee - and Bill Archer – former chairman of the House Ways &Means Committee – published an article in the WSJ on 11/28/2012 stating unfunded government liabilities are $86 Trillion and will bankrupt the government). In history, the harbinger of bad news was likely killed. Politicians don't want to see history repeat itself! To get America back on track, the lies of these politicians need to be exposed along with the facts detailing how these programs are bankrupting the country!

Massive advances in productivity have created enough goods to ensure the basic necessities of life (clothing, food, and shelter) for all Americans. And, the basic necessities of health care (vaccinations, treatment for most known diseases, and emergency assistance for traumatic injury) are affordable. If these government assistance programs were changed to support a more reasonable standard of living for the non-achiever, that would go a long way to solving the future bankruptcy issues confronting the American government. The entitlement programs currently in place provide a lot more than the basic necessities. (Ex. – free cell phone usage, credit to buy expensive sneakers or expensive food products, section 8 housing, college scholarship programs, cancer and heart disease treatment programs, etc.) And, these programs allow able bodied individuals to choose to forego working by simply filing forms to join these give-away programs. It easy to see how the largest of these programs has overwhelmed the ability of the working members of society to produce enough to satisfy the demands of the entitled.

Currently, the U.S. is mortgaging its future production to pay for current and future entitlements. The government is borrowing $300B/year from the Chinese, $250B/year from the Middle Eastern countries, and $500B/year from U.S. worker retirement accounts to help pay for its charity to its 'underprivileged' residents or unfortunate citizens. I believe Americans are smart enough to understand that continuous borrowing to support any life style is unsustainable. I also believe Americans understand bankruptcy has nasty consequences. They should understand that America can't continue down the debt path! With American government debt at these unheard of historically high levels, there is little chance that a painful adjustment can be avoided. However, if that adjustment doesn't happen soon, it will be hard to avoid a second 'Great Depression' in the not too distant future. There is no time to waste. All government spending needs to be cut immediately.

America is in trouble today because Americans have allowed Big Business, Big Labor, and Big Government to become too powerful. It has been in the interests of these entities to promote increased government spending and entitlement policies. It has also been in their interest to promote a devastating free trade and energy policy. For Big Labor, increased government spending means more workers enrolled in unions. More government spending means more demand for Big Business products (and because of lobbying and procurement laws, Big Business gets the lion's share of this increased demand). Big Government is beneficial to politicians whose power keeps growing due to the increasing size of the government purse and due to the growing number of individuals dependent on the government.

The small group of individuals that now control these humungous entities have created the biggest Ponzi scheme in history. They have used borrowing from the American middle class to pay for entitlement programs to gain votes from the poor and the remorseful. They have borrowed to support expensive government programs (coordinated by lobbyist efforts) run by their allies and friends. They have borrowed from the Arabs in support of a poor energy policy. They borrowed trillions (Fannie Mae and Freddie Mac – 2003 to 2008) to support the frenzy in unaffordable home buying. And, now they are cutting the middle class off at the knees by paying middle-class savers one quarter of 1 percentage interest on their savings. They then pass along a low interest rate to help the largest American companies relocate production facilities in China and the developing world to allow slave labor to compete with U.S. labor! In order for the American Dream to stay alive and prosper, this behavior needs to be ended!

Unfortunately, the propaganda machine of the politicians, embraced by the left-wing media, has totally masked the truth from the public. And, the glut of power achieved through entitlement programs has only stimulated our leaders to want more. They are implementing plans to master the energy market by using questions of earth survival to pass massive environmental rules. So, instead of getting out of our reliance on Middle East oil (America has discovered enough resources to power 150 years of future energy needs. We don't need foreign oil!) and the problems associated with our political involvement there, our power structure has chosen to stay with the old policy. Domestic security and the fight against terrorism adds a whole new level of control to those in power (government monitoring of everyone's communication, loss of due process because of threat to American security, hundreds of thousands of security workers hired that now are at the beck and call of the powerful, etc.).

The insatiable power grab doesn't stop with energy. Healthcare has become the next enormous prize. Obamacare was passed in 2010 in spite of huge public protests. Many battles have been fought to reverse this outrageous affront to individual liberty and economic freedom. Yet, with the re-election of President Obama, the momentum to implement this fiscal ball-buster (originally forecast to add $1 trillion to the nation's health cost has now turned into $3 trillion) and liberty extinguisher seems unstoppable.

The American way of life has been subverted by politicians' (and their cohorts) desire for more and more power. The thirst for power has led to deceitful propaganda aimed at tricking the American people. It has led to bad economic and political policy. It has led to subversive actions in regard to the Constitution, the Bill of Rights, and individual freedoms. And, it has put the nation on the doorstep of bankruptcy. In the name of fairness, politicians have abused the compassion of the American people and their willingness to help others. The idea of being good to your neighbors has been contorted into guilt that only good fortune or reprehensible behavior has been responsible for the difference in an individual's standard of living. The original American Dream that hard work and perseverance could lead to a good life by overcoming difficult obstacles has been thrown in the trash bin! Instead, this 'Dream' has been replaced by the notion that individuals are entitled to fruits of the land just because they were born. The last time I looked, the land still had to be worked and cultivated before any fruits could be had!

In order to get America back on the right track, the size and power of the Big Three need to be cut down. The only way to achieve this outcome is first to throw out the politicians voting for more government. Initially, this means voting the Democrats out of control of the Senate in 2014. The voters' message must be clear that they want smaller government in their lives.

Afterwards both the Democratic and the Republican Parties need to be held responsible for their power grab of the last 80 years. The two party system hasn't acted in the best interests of the public because they both have had the same goal of achieving more power. Since these Parties control billions of dollars in the fund raising process for candidates running for office, they have had tremendous power in picking the candidates who were the eventually winners of almost every significant political race (Therefore the candidates that were chosen were beholden to their financiers and obliged to vote for every aspect of their party's agenda. And, that agenda wasn't creating policy in the best interest of America.). The huge cost of political campaigns has reduced the choice of political candidates to those chosen by the two political parties. The political power of the people has thus been marginalized by this circumstance. The current system of campaign financing needs to be overhauled. Chapter 10 will include a discussion of a possible solution.

Once the Democrats are removed from Senate power, the next step required by voters is to force their elected representatives to change the domestic energy policy to one aggressively promoting expansion of incentives for America to become energy independent. At the same time, voters must force their politicians to implement a plan to significantly lower our trade deficit with China and the developing world. Competition with slave labor should not be the reason Americans are losing jobs and America is losing its status as the greatest nation on earth.

Needless to say, the current power structure doesn't want any of these changes to happen. Attempts to unwind their power grab of 80 years will be met with the utmost resistance. Yet, because of the Democrats break with political tradition, which has taken place in the last 8 years, in ending the historic policy of compromise with the Republicans, public action to reduce the two Party power system is more likely to succeed now than in the recent past.

By attacking the Democrats in the 2014 elections for their socialistic policies, voters will be setting the agenda for less government in future elections. It is likely that if the power returns to the Republicans in 2014, the Democrats will return to the old method of compromise with the Republican Party. This will mean political cooperation in trying to retain their 80 years of power consolidation. Before this happens, voters need to be convinced that they have been the pawns of a massive political charade. They need to be convinced that bigness (in business or government) attracts corrupt self-interested power seekers. They need to be convinced that big is bad and self-interest or greed, when leading to increased productivity, is as good for the country as our forefathers had envisioned.

The Tea Party's main agenda concerning the economy and governmental power is to reduce governmental power and maintain a capitalistic economy. It is the logical political organization to take the lead in convincing the public about the evils of socialism and big government. With millions of members and a network structure in place, this political organization can enormously help in the hard task of returning America to the correct path.

Unfortunately, the goals of the Tea Party have been many. Instead of just having one goal of ridding America of socialism, different constituents of the Party have expanded the goals to include social issues such as abortion, illegal immigration, gun control, prayer in schools, etc. This myriad of issues, especially concerning religious issues, has significantly weaken the Party's power. Tea Party members need to realize a weak Party cannot affect change. They need to evaluate the parts of their platform that are not accepted by the general public and eliminate them. Then they need to look for allies. Those allies are America's small entrepreneurs. These small entrepreneurs have the most to lose in a socialistic system. In a socialistic system, the reward of risk-taking is mostly eliminated. With this gone, entrepreneurs will have to give up their life style because the idea that they can be independent and create a better life for their families will be lost. With this in mind, the Tea Party needs to aggressively undertake the task of helping entrepreneurs to organize and form a Small Business Political Party. The coalition of these two groups would definitely swing power to capitalism and conservatism in America.

The immediate objective of this new power base would be convincing the American public that American government needs to be returned to its intended goal of protecting individual independence and freedom. Americans need to be re-educated to believe in the magnificent achievement (the massive increase in the world's standard of living) of capitalism and to want it to continue into the future. And, they need to know that our current huge American government will continue to stifle our country's economy and its citizens' individual freedoms.

This message can be delivered through a massive messaging campaign as well as asking entrepreneurs to discuss the issue of American socialism with their employees. There are 26 million small businesses that employ 80 million Americans. And, the influence of those 26 million owners on their employees could be overwhelming. A unified group of 80 million would be the dominant political force of the country.

To aid in the political re-education of small business employees and society in general, an informative propaganda engine needs to be created. Political ads and guest appearances on radio and TV need to take place explaining the

historic failure of socialism and the need to prevent dominating power structures. These arguments also need to be
presented in forums and discussion groups on the internet.
Challenges to debate well known liberals or socialists should
be constantly issued. High profile liberal news media personalities also need to be persuaded to debate their viewpoint against high profile conservative media personalities
to a national audience. In these debates, a strict moderator
must control the narrative to a discussion of facts and the
underlying assumptions driving the logic of the argument.
Recent so-called debates between opposing party politicians
have been ridiculous as they have resulted in only a rehash
of party talking points with no hard facts or logic presented
in support. The rules should limit debate to the benefits and
the corresponding consequences of socialistic policy vs. capitalistic policy.

The evidence and logic backing the benefits of a capitalistic society vs. a socialistic society are overwhelming. Most
Americans have only heard the rhetoric. The debate of this
issue in the proper format should bolt many Americans out
of the hypnotic trance produced by 50 years of liberal media
and political propaganda. Many liberal voters should be persuaded not to vote for the Democratic platform after hearing
the arguments of the rational side!

Leading up to the 2014 elections, the political competition will come from the Democrats and the liberal media.
The Democratic Party will put their propaganda machine on
full blast. The liberal media dreamers will follow by seeking
out as many heart wrenching stories concerning the poor's

plight at the hands of the self-interested in order to persuade the good-hearted of the need for socialism. Although many borderline liberals would likely be persuaded to vote anti-Democratic due to a media campaign criticizing socialism, most liberals are by definition not critical thinkers. The dreamers will still be believing. And, the Democratic ranks will remain strong.

The Republican Party, still stinging from the political treachery of the Democratic Party, will initially be allies of a coalition composed of the Tea Party and small businesses. However, there will be battles in the primaries concerning the Tea Party's Coalition candidates and the Republican Party's candidates. This is already happening and will likely become more heated. Unfortunately, this conflict will likely open the door for Democrats to retain power in 2014. Primary (election) conflict is what likely caused conservative voters to withhold their vote in 2012 and may result in the same action in 2014. Unless the Tea Party's strength is magnified many times in the next year, they would be wise to reserve political primary battles to only the Tea Party's sure winners until 2016. If the Tea Party is able to massively organize small businesses in an alliance with them, future elections will be much more fruitful.

The American Dream can only be saved if Democrats are tossed out of the Senate majority in 2014. Then, the 2016 elections must be won by the Tea Party's coalition with a Small Business Party. The achievement of these goals will allow a change in policy concerning America's energy policy and also its free trade policy.

It will also create a political environment that advocates returning power to the people by creating rules to encourage Big Business and Big Labor to reduce their size. It will bring back jobs to America, increase productivity and encourage the American work ethic. The new power structure will also protect the tremendous assets of our country from foreign plunder.

CHAPTER 10

Conclusion

America is in trouble. America is up to its eyeballs in debt. The visible debt is $17 trillion. The hidden debt of unfunded liabilities is another $60 to $70 trillion. With a population of 316 million, the debt burden of each American (including children) is $54 thousand at $17 trillion or $275 thousand at $87 trillion. Our politicians have led us to this outcome by lying about how a rich America could afford to take care of its citizens from cradle to grave and from sickness to health. They told us all that was needed were government rules to divest the rich of their ill gotten wealth.

The belief in this propaganda has led to the massive growth in Big Government. Big Labor followed closely behind switching from negotiating for private industry workers to government workers. Big Labor's efforts had led to American companies being uncompetitive. New industries and foreign competition led to massive corporate failures as the unreasonably high wages negotiated by the unions led many businesses (auto, steel, clothing, etc.) to bankruptcy. Union membership plummeted with these failures in private industry.

The opportunity to organize government workers however blossomed. Governmental unions basked in the opportunity that big government never could go bankrupt regardless of sky high demands. And, negotiating high salaries and benefits was much easier as the public administrators negotiating the other side had a huge public trough to suck from with generally no counter-balance of cost restraint such as profitability.

On the business front, businesses were allowed to grow to enormous sizes. Foreign competition was often used as the excuse not to enact anti-trust regulation. Also, Big Business fit the bill for politicians to get paid for their influence (Interestingly, all politicians holding high office become multi-millionaires after their public service). Big Business could afford to hire former government officials and lobby for lucrative government projects. Small businesses were not considered for these contracts because size was determined by high level officials to be a risk factor. The American public's massive problem with pork barrel projects and lobbying is a direct result of the cozy relation between Big Government and Big Business.

The power of the Big Three working together have determined economic and political policy in recent years. When owners managed their own businesses instead of elite managers, there was much more concern about the long-term effects of government policy on their businesses and society. About 40 years ago, elite managers started to control the business world, not the owners. They were paid to take risk with other people's money. They won when they were right but the owners lost when they're wrong. And, winning in the short run (ex. - betting on the housing bubble) was often not a long-term winning strategy. The short-term winning strategy was often determined by following government policy.

This path has led to policies in the interests of the powerful, not the general population. America is in crisis because of it.

When it comes to the Big Three, bigness is bad in America. The corruption it has produced stands out like a sore thumb. And, for the obvious reason, nothing is done about it. The change the American public voted for in 2008 is desperately needed. Unfortunately, the country was misled. Americans wanted less power in Big Government and Big Business, not more. They wanted their politicians to cleanse the government and its corrupt relation to big business. Instead, they got sold a bill of goods while elected representatives enhanced this practice instead of eliminating it.

America needs to elect politicians that will reduce the size of government by voting to reduce the government's budget. It needs politicians to vote to shift many programs such as education, health care and welfare either to the state and local level or to the private sector. It also needs to develop incentive programs for government workers to help eliminate fraud and abuse (Currently, fraud and abuse cause the government to hire more workers. Our politicians are happy with a bigger government, so there is a disincentive for government employees to report fraud as it may result in a smaller budget and a smaller government work force).

America also needs its politicians to produce laws that incentivize big businesses to reduce their size. Big businesses are much less efficient than small businesses. Yet, they survive by the power of their size. Big business can afford massive marketing campaigns to persuade customers to buy its products. They can influence other big businesses not to buy product from small companies because of the risk of doing business with small companies. The interconnected network of elite professionals have incentives to do business between themselves in order to crowd out smaller competitors. Government regulation puts a much higher burden on small business because this cost represents a much bigger percentage of revenue. There are a vast number of other criteria that make competition with big business extremely difficult. Small businesses only survive by creating much superior products at a much more efficient level. That's why 70% of all new jobs created in last 30 years have come from small businesses.

The fact that business gets less efficient as it gets bigger would imply that government policy should discourage this outcome. Big companies should be encouraged to divest themselves of multiple businesses that have no synergies with each other. Spin-offs should be encouraged by a new graduated tax on total corporate revenues above a prescribed level that defines a large conglomerate. This tax on revenues would cause shareholders to insist on divestiture of subsidiaries as it would reduce tax liabilities. Historically, the stock market has significantly rewarded spin-offs (divestitures) as they have enhanced efficiency and profitability of the combined companies.

In addition to encouraging spin-offs, a similar tax policy to encourage downsizing of giant corporations in any particular industry should also be considered. In this case, a divestiture of similar assets could also lead to public and shareholder benefit. The power (based on revenue) of the elite management teams of big businesses would be lessened with this tax policy. This would be beneficial to shareholders and workers as the enhanced competitiveness with new leadership would increase the total enterprise value of both entities (vs. the pre-spinoff company) while increasing new job opportunities.

Some critics may argue that the capitalistic system has a built-in mechanism to produce the most efficient corporate structure and therefore has no need for any government interference. Unfortunately, a true capitalistic market currently doesn't exist. As discussed earlier in this book, large corporations are being run not solely for shareholder benefit but for their management's benefit as well.

Lastly, politicians need to introduce laws to reduce the power of Big Labor. Reducing the size of government would play a significant role in reducing the size of Big Labor. In addition, imposing a government fee structure that increases with the size of union membership, similar to the one proposed for businesses, would go a long way to lessen the power of Big Labor.

These initiatives to decentralize power would revitalize the American Dream. The major sticking point is the current process of electing politicians. As described earlier, America's two party system controls this process. Today, political candidates can only win with access to massive amounts of money. And, fund raising is dominated by the Democratic and Republican party. The donors are chiefly Big Business and Big Labor. Very wealthy Americans closely associated with these two entities also are a factor. A new method of fund raising and candidate selection needs to be instituted to change the current power structure.

Social media and the internet have produced profound change in the behavior of the American consumer. It is logical that these communications networks could also impact American politics to the same degree. By combining social media with the entertainment industry, a new method of introducing potential candidates to the public could be created. Americans have shown great interest in TV shows that have educational benefit. They are exasperated by the current political process as they feel impotent in effecting change through that process. The right chemistry of the new media, TV, and public interest in politics could lead to a process that changes the dynamics of the current political selection process (The author is in the process of trying to put together such an effort. Interested readers should go to *www.changebiggovernment.com* to learn more).

America needs the right leaders in order to return to greatness. These leaders need to come out of the alliance of a new party formed by a coalition between the Tea Party and small business entrepreneurs. The platform of this alliance must be to enlighten the public of the failure of the current government while also informing them of the perils of concentrated power. The initial goal of these new leaders needs to be removing the Democrats from power in the Senate in 2014. The next goal needs to be electing a significant number of their own candidates to influential political positions in 2016. With adequate political power, the agenda of making America energy independent could be implemented. Also, the devastating free trade agenda could be changed to one designed for fair trade. The final goal of the coalition should be changing the election process to one that is not solely dependent on a fund raising process that leads to compromised politicians.

The author of this book believes the greatness of America can be restored only by its people, not by its current leadership. This book is written in hopes that the mystical friendly mask of government created by leftist mainstream media and leftist educators will be ripped off by exposing either their ignorance or their lies. The author also hopes conservative Americans will rethink their positive opinions about Big Business and the Republican Party. America is close to the point of no return. Both major political parties have failed us. The Democrats are about to close the door on 200 years of freedom. And, the Republicans are following close behind. Once this come to pass, what country will nourish mankind's hopes for freedom and the pursuit of happiness? Freedom and the American Dream will have died. Americans need to act before it's too late.

CHAPTER 11

Reader's Interaction Requested

Risking the appearance of supreme arrogance, the author has created a website for interaction with the reader. The author is interested in whether America's appetite for change is enough to motivate a response against the country's current economic and political policy.

Please go to *http://www.changebiggovernment.com/*. There will be no requests for money or identification. Votes for opinions will be requested. And, results will be published. Also, a social network will be available for the more concerned.

The author is publishing this book in hopes that it may stimulate its readers to action. Our political and economic systems need to be changed. Americans need to act now to preserve our incredible way of life.

APPENDIX FOR STATISTICS

Page 1:
http://rt.com/usa/half-government-million-percent-320/
http://www.heritage.org/research/reports/2013/11/the-2013-index-of-dependence-on-government
• Government dependency

Page 30:
http://www.usgovernmentspending.com/percent_gdp
http://www.usgovernmentspending.com/total_1930USpt_15ps5n
• Government spending as a % of GDP - 1930

Page 38:
http://www.usgovernmentspending.com/total_1999USpt_15ps5n

http://www.usgovernmentspending.com/year_spending_1999USbn_15bs2n#usgs302

http://www.usgovernmentspending.com/year_spending_2011USbn_15bs2n#usgs302

http://www.usgovernmentspending.com/total_2008USrt_15rs5n

http://www.usgovernmentspending.com/total_2008USpt_15ps5n

http://www.usgovernmentspending.com/total_2012USrt_15rs5n

http://www.usgovernmentspending.com/total_2012USpt_15ps5n

• Government spending - total and as a % of GDP - 1999, 2011
• Government Spending, GDP Change - 2008, 2012

Page 39:
*http://www.politifact.com/virginia/statements/2011/dec/30/
eric-cantor/cantor-says-small-businesses-create-70-percent-
us-/*

• Small business job creation

Page 46:
*http://www.usgovernmentspending.com/year_spending_
2009USbn_15bs2n#usgs302*

*http://www.usgovernmentspending.com/year_spending_
2013USbn_15bs2n#usgs302*
• Government debt - 2009, 2013

Page 54:
*http://www.examiner.com/article/apple-shares-soar-as-
employees-china-passes-500-000*
• Apple jobs in China

http://prospect.org/article/plight-american-manufacturing
• Lost manufacturing jobs

*http://www.census.gov/foreign-trade/statistics/historical/
gands.txt*
• Trade deficit statistics

Page 56:
*http://www.census.gov/foreign-trade/statistics/historical/
gands.txt*
• Oil imports

Page 56:
http://useconomy.about.com/od/tradepolicy/p/us-china-trade.
htm
- China trade deficit

Page 58:
http://filipspagnoli.wordpress.com/stats-on-human-rights/
statistics-on-gross-domestic-product-correlations/#48
- Energy usage and the standard of living

Page 59:
http://data.worldbank.org/indicator/NY.GDP.PCAP.
CD?page=3
- China and U.S. personal income

Page 85:
www.gallup.com/poll/125645/socialism-viewed-positively-
americans.aspx
- Americans viewpoint on socialism